Nip It

Stop Negativity
Moment by Moment

Kristen Fredricks
Jeanie Wade

Krispective

Krispective, Inc.
www.krispective.com

ISBN: 978-1-940922-10-2

Dedication

While writing this book, Kris lost her mother and Jeanie lost her father. They each passed away within three months of us deciding to work on this project. Writing a book about dealing with negative moments helped both of us through some difficult times and sad moments. During these past two years, our surviving parents, Cora Wade and Jerry Staub, have shown strength and resiliency. We dedicate this book to them.

To Jerry Staub, thank you for all your support during this project, as well as throughout my whole life. I am blessed to have you as my father. You and mom helped me build this positive attitude about life, and for that, I am forever thankful.

> Love,
> Kris

To Cora Wade, thank you for being my mother, my friend, and a great source of inspiration and support. You helped me to see that women could be and do anything, as long as they believed in it. I'm glad that I have had you in my life through the years.

> Love,
> Jeanie

Contents

Acknowledgments

We would like to thank all of our friends and family who helped and supported us through the writing and publishing process. We could not have done this without you. The following people deserve special thanks:

Gary Fredricks, for your technical expertise, support, and encouragement. You helped take our draft and turn this into a real book! You believed in us from day one, when we came home and announced to you that we would be writing a book. Your confidence in our success has never wavered and you have done everything possible to support us on our path.

Christina Mandolfo, Lisa Nuwer, Heather Waterman, for your patience and feedback during the very first review cycle of the book. As the chapters were e-mailed sporadically, you never complained, and you always had a positive way to give us tough feedback. You truly helped us shape the book.

Donna (Wade) Doak and Dawn (Wade) Roberts, by the time you reviewed the book, we had been working on it for eighteen months. We were getting tired, but your feedback and encouragement uplifted us and propelled us through to the end.

Chris Woodyard, for sharing your knowledge about how to write a book, and for directing us to the important literary resources we needed to take this book from an idea to a reality.

Bill Romans, thirteen years ago you recruited Jeanie to come and work with you and Kris. You knew we would make a great team so you arranged for us to work together. You were right! Not only did we make a great work team, but we have a friendship now that will last a lifetime. You have altered both of our lives forever. We do not know where this journey of book writing will take us, but we have you to credit for bringing us together to let us have this opportunity.

Michael Mandolfo, for the photo of Kristen Fredricks. Thank you for your support and encouragement, not only during the photo shoot but through this whole project.

Dave McIntosh, of Dave McIntosh Photographics, for the photo of Jeanie Wade. Thanks for such a positive and fun photo session.

Susan Leonard, for taking our rough ideas and creating a cover that really captures the essence of the book.

Ilene Stankiewicz, for taking the time to understand our goals and editing the book to make the end product much better.

Each of you has left a lasting imprint on this book, as well as in our hearts. We are so thankful for your support!

Preface

The Journey Begins

Sometimes in life you make a decision and then you receive a sign it was the right one. That's exactly what happened to us in December of 2011. While Christmas shopping, we decided we would write a book together, and immediately after making that decision, we saw the following sign in the entranceway of a store:

"Go confidently in the direction of your dreams! Live the life you've imagined."

– Henry David Thoreau

At that moment, we knew we were on the right path. Over the upcoming weeks, we brainstormed ideas and themes for the book. We planned for the focus to be on keeping a positive attitude, centered on what we fondly call "Krisisms."

What are Krisisms? Kris has a habit of scrambling or misquoting common sayings into what we coined as "Krisisms," such as "nip it in the butt." You're probably asking yourself what kind of expression is that? Allow us to explain the history of that expression and how, ultimately, this book was titled and written. Our journey begins with Kris.

My name is Kristen Fredricks. My dear friend and coauthor is Jeanie Wade. Jeanie and I worked together for many years in Western New York until Jeanie was transferred to Maryland in 2006. We are not famous psychologists or self-help gurus. We do not have English degrees and we are not literary buffs. We are your average forty-plus-year-old women (one a "kid mom" and one a "dog mom"), who are often characterized as being a dynamic duo. And as such, we each bring different strengths to this book.

I am a wife, mother, and career woman. I enjoy hiking, skiing, and reading. My husband Gary, my seven-year-old son Matthew, and my four-year-old daughter Sara make my life exciting. I have been described as sincere, caring, and an extremely positive person. I am often told, "You are one of the most positive people I know," and once, during an evaluation at work, my boss told me I was "almost positive to a fault."

Over ten years ago, I was making a presentation to a large group of supervisors at a meeting focused on reviewing compliance procedures. I told the management team how crucial it was to follow processes and remain compliant to the company's procedures. If anyone were to observe an employee who did not follow process, I advised them to "please 'nip it in the butt' early."

Jeanie, my boss at the time, took me aside after the presentation and said, "Did you realize you said 'nip it in the butt?'" I was decidedly relaxed about it and replied, "Yes." Jeanie then went on to explain that the expression is "nip it in the bud," which means to stop a small problem before it gets big.

"So does 'nip it in the butt,'" I said. "Why would nipping something in the bud stop someone from doing something? If they got nipped in the butt, now that would actually get their attention!" At the time, Jeanie laughed, and she eventually learned that I had many of these "isms." So many, in fact, Jeanie started a list of "isms," which led us to write this book.

Jeanie's list of Krisisms—those mixed up phrases—has given us many laughs through the years. The "Krisism" tag caught on, and my coworkers, friends, and husband started noticing when I said them. Another one of the Krisisms was "flip the tables" instead of "turn the tables."

Years ago, Jeanie and I were brainstorming on how to solve a problem regarding negativity in the workplace. I said, "We have to find a way to flip the tables for this team." Of course, Jeanie had to stop and try to explain that the correct expression is "turn the tables." My answer to this one was "turning the tables seems so soft and passive. If someone flipped the table in front of you, wouldn't that grab your attention?"

After Jeanie moved to Baltimore and took a new job, anytime I said a Krisism, someone would e-mail Jeanie to let her know the latest phrase. She would update the list and take the opportunity to resend it to the gang. Following every new "ism," there were always a few e-mails back and forth teasing me about the latest phrase or even commenting on one of the former Krisisms. I always said that the joke would be on them when I wrote a book about my "isms" and I became famous.

A few years prior to starting this actual book, I drafted an outline of chapter titles and determined the book would be about my life's perspective via Krisisms. But I never got around to writing it. Life was too hectic, and at the time, I just couldn't envision that someone else would want to read what I wrote about staying positive in life.

That outlook changed in the fall of 2011. At work, we were going through the third round of layoffs in two years. I was struggling with the knowledge that my job could be in jeopardy, and the jobs of people I had worked with for almost eighteen years were hanging in the balance. I was doing a lot of soul-searching about my life and how I wanted my future to look. I loved my job, and I felt like I made a difference every day, but the future was extremely uncertain. During that turbulent time, I knew I needed to maintain my positive attitude and stay true to my primary core beliefs:

❀   It will all work out.

❀   Everything happens for a reason.

I started believing that if I could share my "fault" of extreme positivity with at least one person and make a difference in their life, then writing an "ism" book would all be worth it. I also predicted that if I was focused on writing a book about positives, then the writing would help me stay positive during this dark period at work. In a way, it would be therapy. As it turned out, within three months of deciding to write this book, some significant life changing events occurred in both my and Jeanie's lives. Focusing on the "nip it" and "flip it" theme helped us to see things in a different light.

With this newfound energy, I began thinking about the book several times each day. In the shower, or on a walk, I would think about what subjects might lend themselves to the book. I had a lot of ideas floating around in my head, but I never took pen to paper or fingers to keyboard to get them documented.

That all changed on a Friday evening in November of 2011. The kids were in bed, my husband Gary had fallen asleep on the couch, and I was alone watching Piers Morgan interview Mickey Roarke. Roarke was talking about having a second chance in life and taking it. It felt as if he was speaking directly to me. I stood up, walked to the computer, and found my draft of the chapter titles for my "ism" book. Then, I just started typing. All sorts of ideas were flowing. I was in a "zone," and I knew I was meant to write a book. At that moment, I made a commitment to myself that I would finish the book by the end of 2012. On that same night, I decided my goal was to publish the book and get at least one letter from one person who said something to the effect of, "Your book made me laugh, and it made me look at life differently." At that point, all my effort would be worth it.

I worked on the book for a few weeks, and surprisingly, I got nowhere. I remember thinking maybe this is what writer's block is. But how could I have writer's block? I had only just started. I had lots of ideas, but nothing seemed to fit or flow well. I couldn't create a theme out of what I was writing. In my heart, something was clearly missing. Jeanie visited my family and me in early December 2011 for the holidays. While we were between shops during a Christmas shopping spree, the "aha" moment of what was missing hit me. I realized it was Jeanie! It was time for her to join the journey.

❀ ❀ ❀ ❀ ❀

My name is Jeanie Wade and Kris is right about how on that snowy December night, we made a pact to turn her dream of writing a positivity book into a reality. It all sounded exciting, but there were definitely some challenges. For one, I live near Baltimore, Maryland about 350 miles from Kris. I am very busy with my three wonderful adopted dogs: Ditto, a beagle/terrier mix; Webster, a golden retriever/black lab mix; and Sidney, an English setter. Keeping me even busier is my passion, volunteering for Hero Dogs, Inc., a nonprofit that raises and trains service dogs for wounded and disabled veterans. And I'll be honest, I thought Kris was crazy, however, her enthusiasm is contagious, and if anyone else had asked me, I would have said no. Yet it was Kris asking, and the idea sounded intriguing, so I agreed to be part of this project. But then reality hit. With my busy life, and Kris' busy life with two young kids and an adventurous husband, how were we going to write a book long-distance?

Well, here is where Kris' eternal optimism (we can do it!) and my practical realism (here's how we can do it) kicked in. We decided not to put too much pressure on ourselves and vowed to have fun on this project. We chose to spend every Sunday evening together on the phone working on the book. We had some great laughs and some sad moments, vented our frustrations, and just enjoyed the ride. Interestingly, I had it set in my mind that I was going to do all I could to help Kris realize her dream, and before I knew it, it had become my dream, too!

I began to believe in Kris' mantra that "everything happens for a reason" and soon realized that I brought a different perspective to the book than Kris did. Kris and I are decidedly different, and we often have different perspectives on situations. As Kris said, she is a naturally positive person. When I first met Kris, I didn't even know what positive energy was. She taught me, and now I am in tune with the impact that negative people and negative energy can have on our lives. I am not a naturally positive person like Kris, but I am also not an inherently negative person.

I like to think that I am fairly typical, and even tend to be a bit skeptical. Yet over the years, I have learned about, seen, and lived how Kris' philosophy of staying positive works in the real world. Being positive doesn't come as easily to me as it does to Kris. Yet I now "practice" positivity every day. For those of you who are skeptical or not sure this will work for you personally, I am here to tell you that it can and does.

I am committed to getting this message out to everyone so they can experience the same awakening to positivity that I did. If a typical person like me can come to learn and practice positivity, then anyone can. So, I was happy to take part in writing this book, and on that December night, I decided to embark on this journey with Kris.

We hope we grabbed your attention with our first "Krispective" title, based on the original Krisism, "nip it in the butt." Our intention is to help you identify those negative moments in your life and provide some guidance on how to nip that negativity in the butt. By stopping negativity moment by moment, you can stop creating negative thought patterns, behaviors, or beliefs. This can lead to a happier life for you and those around you.

Aristotle was quoted as saying, "Anything that we have to learn to do, we learn by the actual doing of it. We become just by doing just acts, temperate by doing temperate ones, brave by doing brave ones." As he pointed out, we learn by doing, and this is certainly true of removing negativity from our lives. We become more positive by acting positively. This does not always come easily or naturally for us as complex humans. Especially when we consider that negativity can come from so many places, including what people say about us, what we think, the situations we are in, or just from our interactions with other people.

How can we avoid this negativity in our lives? We must choose to be positive. Yes, positivity is a choice, a choice that comes naturally to some, but most of us have to work at being positive. We must make a conscious decision to be positive and then proceed to practice this ability. This unique perspective on life, or "Krispective" as we call it, is what we apply to our lives almost every day. Through our 'spectives, we hope this book will help you learn about your own perspective and to begin or continue your personal journey to a more positive life. Life is too short not to find joy and positivity every day. Thank you for choosing to read our book. Have fun!

Kristen Fredricks and Jeanie Wade

Chapter 1

Introduce It

The Journey Begins

You are about to begin a journey of learning how to "nip it" and "flip it." What is the "it" we are talking about? "It" is simply a negative moment, person, or situation that you are faced with at any point in your life. And just what do we mean by "nip it" and "flip it"? To "nip it" is to stop the negativity from growing. And to "flip it" means turning the negative situation around into something more positive. For example, how do you feel when…

the dog eats your shoe?
the kids dump cereal on the kitchen floor?
you get a flat tire driving to work?
you drop a glass jar of pickles at the grocery store?
someone in the parking lot takes your parking spot?
a team member at work doesn't pull their weight?
someone cuts in front of you in the line at the deli?
a fellow worker criticizes you?

Do you get a twinge in your stomach? Do you curse? Do you yell? Does your head hurt? Do you cry? Reactions like these most likely indicate you are dealing with something negative.

And how about when you interact with people? Do you find that some leave you energized and others sap your energy? Do you understand why different people affect you differently? Have you ever found yourself dreading going somewhere but you weren't quite sure what caused that feeling? This learning adventure will show you how to shift those negative moments in your life so that they will appear to be more positive.

We're going to help you explore all of those questions and provide you with the tools to transform your everyday negative moments. The techniques are simple to apply, and with some practice, will become habit. If you choose to implement some of our suggestions, you'll be able to change your overall attitude about life, which can help you feel more at peace on a daily basis.

We won't be taking on bigger, life-changing moments. You know, those moments that have a profound impact on you—the loss of someone close, a fear that stops you from doing something, an illness that impacts your life in ways you could never imagine, etc. We'll tackle some of those bigger moment topics in a future book. For now, we're focusing on stopping, or "nipping" the negative energy in smaller moments.

Negativity is a normal part of life, but how can we minimize it and stop these negative experiences in their tracks, or as Kris likes to say, "Nip them in the butt"? The steps we use to deal with negativity every day is illustrated in the following graphic.

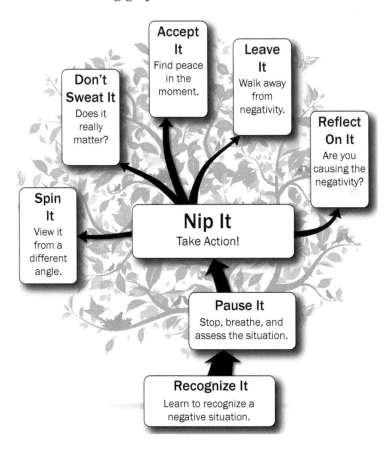

First, and most importantly, is to learn to recognize "it," the negativity, because it isn't always obvious. Second, pause so you can minimize your emotional responses and decide how best to deal with the negativity. Then it's time to take action and "nip it."

Learn how to "nip it" and "flip the tables" on those negative thoughts, people, and situations to either make them positive or at least neutral. There are many different techniques to nip the negativity and flip the tables of a negative moment. We have dedicated a chapter to each of these topics:

✿ **Spin It** - View the situation from a different angle. Try to find the positive in the negative moment.

✿ **Don't Sweat It** - Assess whether the negative situation really matters in the grand scheme of life.

✿ **Accept It** - Accept that the situation is negative; you can't change it, and find peace in the moment.

✿ **Leave It** - Walk away from negative situations and people.

✿ **Reflect on It** - Determine if you are causing negativity in your own life.

No matter how positive a person you are, negativity can show up at any moment in your life. Your reaction to the situation determines how the negative moment will affect you.

Throughout the book, we'll present real-life examples of everyday negative situations to illustrate these concepts. As you read through the pages, think of your own experiences with negativity and how you handled them. The more you apply these nipping and flipping concepts, the easier it will be to keep positivity in your life. We hope as you read through the book, you will walk away with some ideas that you can apply to your next negative situation and to the rest of your life.

Chapter 2

Recognize It

Identify Negative Moments

If you are going to nip negativity, then you first need to be able to recognize it. What we view as negative may be different from what you view as negative. How can that be? Here are a few examples to illustrate our point:

❀ You may think a rainy day is negative. We like rainy days because they help the flowers grow.

❀ You may view a certain politician as negative while

we view that same person as a realist.

❀ Not getting a certain job may be extremely disappointing for you, but we may view it as a chance to find a better job.

❀ Having an argument with someone at work may disrupt your entire day, but the other person may not even realize it was an argument.

Every moment, every interaction, every conversation we have has a chance to be experienced as positive or negative. Once you begin to recognize the negative moments, you can begin to change your reaction to them and truly impact your life.

The first step in recognizing that you are being faced with a negative moment is to become aware of how you feel when it happens. This awareness fine-tunes what we refer to as your "negative vibe indicators," which can be either physical or emotional. As you become more aware, sometimes you will know you are in a negative moment just by how you feel, not by assessing the situation around you. The sooner you feel that negativity, the earlier you can "nip it in the butt!"

Let's start to work on this. Tomorrow, with every interaction you have with someone, take a few seconds to think about the emotions you are feeling.

❀ Does the clerk at the store make you feel happy?

❀ When your boss comes to talk to you, do you feel anxious and wish he/she would leave?

❀ Do you feel sad after a conversation with a friend?

❀ Do you feel angry or upset with a co-worker?

❀ Does your significant other provide you with a positive outlook on a certain situation?

❀ How does your physical body feel with each interaction?

- Are you laughing?

- Are you gritting your teeth?

- Are you smiling?

- Does your stomach hurt?

- Does your head throb?

- Do you feel more tired?

- Do you feel more energized?

Once you form the habit of being aware of the feelings that other people and situations evoke within you, you'll be prepared to counter negative people and situations. And once you recognize it, you're ready to deal with it.

In this chapter, we'll show you some examples of moments we viewed as negative and how people felt and reacted in those situations. We're all human and sometimes we get caught up in a not so positive situation. Sometimes we fall into a negative spiral, and you may say or do things that are not quite as positive as we'd like them to be. We allow negativity to nip us in the butt. It's inevitable. It happens to all of us.

However, after you learn to recognize "it," you can choose to react differently in negative moments and change your attitude and outcomes. For instance, in the first story, Kris' husband Gary had a negative experience that caused him to stay grumpy most of the day. He knew he was upset, he knew he was in a negative moment, but he couldn't pull himself out of it. Have you had an experience like that? Did you understand what caused it? Did you even consider trying to nip it?

What Did the Chairs Do to You?

By Kris

On our way home from a camping week-end years ago, Gary and I passed a hardware store that was selling outdoor chairs. We had been talking about getting them for our patio, so we decided to pull in and buy them. We were only about thirty minutes from home, and it would be a perfect way to end our mini vacation; relaxing on our patio in some new chairs with a drink and maybe a book or newspaper. Note: This was clearly before kids. Now we only have time to skim the newspaper and dream about relaxing.

We bought two chairs and Gary loaded them onto the roof of our Jeep. The ride home was uneventful, and the chairs stayed right in place. Well, that is until we got home. We pulled into the garage,and heard a loud crunch. Picture the noise that resin chairs make when they are slammed into a wall. It is, actually, pretty loud.

We both were surprised and looked at each other with intrigue."What was that?"we said in unison. Almost instantly we both realized what happened. Ironically, I thought it was kind of funny, and even let out a little giggle.

Gary didn't find it that funny. There were pieces of resin chair everywhere. He let out a few choice words and then proceeded to pick up a piece of the chair and bang it on a nearby tree. When that piece was broken into many smaller pieces, he went for another one. I tried telling him it was okay, and we could get some new chairs. No one was hurt and the garage wasn't damaged. The only things to meet their demise were the chairs. No big deal. We could relax in other chairs or we could tackle the unpacking and laundry.

Gary stayed in a funk most of the afternoon. There was nothing I could say to snap him out of his mood; he needed to sulk. Sometimes that's the only way to process the negativity. When he finally was ready to talk, he admitted he was angry because he felt stupid. My response was, "Everyone makes mistakes. I also forgot they were on the roof." He then proceeded to tell me this was actually the second time he had done something like this. The first time was at a bank drive-through when he was in college, with his bike on the top of his Blazer.

Now at this point, I truly only saw the humor in the situation and broke out laughing. Watching him crash his bike into a bank drive-through must have been a sight for the other customers! In that case, no one was hurt except Gary's pride, and there was no damage except to the bike.

Gary learned a few lessons from these accidents and designed a taller garage door in our new house to avoid losing items from the car roof! I guess if you know what might send you in a negative spiral, do what it takes to make sure that negative moment doesn't happen again!

Think about your lost battles with negativity and reflect on them to see if there is a trend as to their causes. If there is, you will be able to beat the negativity over time in those

types of situations. You will begin to understand your trigger points and perhaps even learn to avoid the situations entirely. Having awareness is a big step in the right direction to more positive moments.

Once you become aware of how you feel in negative moments, you will recognize them more quickly and begin to understand your reactions. At that point, you can work on your reaction to those moments to nip the negativity. In the following story, the negativity kept piling up, and Kris never even knew what hit her until it was too late. If her negative vibe indicators had been fine-tuned that day, she would have been able to avoid the entire situation.

Holiday Craziness

By Kris

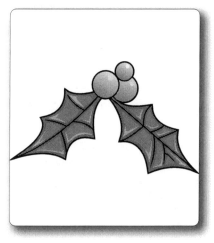

Despite how positive I can normally be, I surely slip into the negative spiral from time to time. In hindsight, it is normally something I will laugh at, but in the moment I can be a crazy lady. One of the best stories to illustrate this comes from Christmas Eve 2011. I can sum it up for you in one sentence. And, if that's enough for you, you can skip to the end.

Negativity nipped me in the butt so hard that I made my five year-old niece Meagan cry on Christmas Eve!

What kind of aunt makes her niece cry on Christmas Eve, one of the most exciting holidays of all times for children? Isn't this the holiday where joy and spirit are flowing, and everyone is happy?

Let me set the stage: every Christmas Eve my sister, Kara and I, and our respective families head to my parents' house for presents, dinner, and more presents. In 2011, Kara's three children were six, five and three. My two children were five and two. All five of our children are high energy on normal days. So on Christmas Eve, they have the combined energy of the rockets launching the space shuttle.

It's thrilling to see the wonder and excitement in their eyes and listen to their anticipation for what Santa will bring. It's hectic and a lot of fun, and that makes for many incredible memories that we have shared together over the years. However, the frenzy can create a little stress for all the adults present, and if you aren't fully grounded and armed for the craziness, it can throw you off your positivity game. It happens to the best of us.

My mother loved holidays and loved giving presents to the kids. Ever since I was little, the tree was always overflowing with presents and the gift opening was nonstop. This gift opening fury certainly ratchets up the whole energy of the house. Add some junk food, soda, and cookies to the kids, and now we are a train wreck waiting to happen. Santa himself probably would avoid the house when we are at the peak of our Christmas Eve festivities.

After a few hours, my sister and I realized we needed to get some solid food in the kids. Mom was in charge of dinner. She always preferred being alone in the kitchen to deal with dinner preparations. I am sure it was her chance to get some peace and quiet on busy occasions like Christmas Eve. She had her own way of doing things and undoubtedly had her own schedule. We all knew never to rush a dinner; she had her own timetable, and that was just how it was.

Somehow, Kara convinced me to enter the kitchen and encourage mom to move things along. At the time, I thought it was a good idea. I assumed she would understand. The kids were wound up and hungry. What I didn't factor in was that Mom had been nipped by all the commotion, and the negativity was building up in her. I think the noise and craziness had worn on her a bit. Let's just say my interruption was less than welcomed by her. But she tried hard to let me help.

Yet, very quickly I realized my help was not perceived as help. But I had a one-track mind: Get the kids some food before one of them has a meltdown. One meltdown can cause a domino effect. We could very well end up with five meltdowns. There is no returning from that. Trust me. We have experienced a multi-meltdown a few times in our family.

As I was trying to help, I was met with criticism at every turn. And, of course, her criticism was met with a snotty remark from me. Remember, Mom had already been nipped and I was working hard to stop the kids from losing it. We were definitely not working together as a team. As you see from the snippets of conversation, we continued to escalate each other's negative vibes.

§

Mom: "Why did you get those plates out? Those are plain dinner plates, not Christmas dinner plates."

Kris: "If you wanted Christmas plates out, why did you put these on top?"

§

Mom: "Don't use the regular napkins, I have nice Christmas napkins."

Kris: "Those fancy napkins are useless. They don't actually clean."

Mom: "I don't care. I bought them and we are using them."

Kris: "Yes, that makes sense; five messy kids with napkins that look good but don't clean."

§

Mom: "You can't use that as a salad serving spoon. I need that for the beans."

Kris: "Then why don't we just use the bean spoon for the salad spoon?"

Mom: "Don't be ridiculous. That will never work."

§

Mom: "You just gave the kids regular glasses? You know I have Christmas glasses."

Kris: "Yes, but the Christmas ones are glass and I didn't think that was a good choice for the little ones."

Mom: "Well if the kids were better behaved, we could give them glass."

§

Mom: "The way you put the chairs at the table won't give people room to get in or out; you need to stagger them."

Kris: "If you would let me set up the card
             table, there would be no space issue."

Mom: "I need the card table for the appetizers."

Kris: "Mom, it's almost dinner time. We are
             done with the appetizers."

Mom: "Oh, yeah? I see one of the kids eating
             a cheese puff right now. Obviously, they
             aren't done."

Kris: "That's because they're hungry and we
             don't have dinner ready for them!"

We carried on this way for about thirty minutes. The bickering included where each person would sit, where the pickles would go, and who should have the meat in front of them. For those of you women reading this book, you may be able to relate to this. Sometimes our relationships with our moms are funny. We love each other dearly, but boy can we wind each other up.

During those lovely thirty minutes, I was continually approached by children whining to me about how hungry they were and wanting to know when they would get to open the next present. Little hands kept reaching up to the table and snatching bits of food. Of course, every snatch left a trail of crumbs, pickle juice, or sauce on the floor. Having to clean up behind them during this was just making me ripe for the nipping.

My next step was to try and decide the best seating arrangement for everyone. Based on prior experience, Kara and I have learned the best approach is to sit a child in between two adults. Some children have better manners based on which adult they sit next to. Whoever sits next to Grandpa is normally the best behaved, because he doesn't tolerate anything.

I finally figure it out after multiple changes from Mom and in walks my niece—my unsuspecting, hungry, beautiful, five-year-old, sweet niece. She gently asks me where she would sit. I pointed to her seat, which was right in front of where I was standing. Then she asks where her mom was sitting. I pointed across the table from where I was standing. Her mom was going to sit between the two eldest boys to help keep them from being too disruptive.

My niece didn't like that answer. She said, "I want to sit next to Mommy." All she wanted was to have dinner next to her mom. No big deal, right? It could have been an easy fix. All I had to do was swap two adults around. But remember, I had just spent thirty minutes bickering with my mother and playing defense to all the kids coming into the eating area. My niece telling me she wanted a change was the straw. You know the straw I'm talking about? The one that breaks your back, and you lose all rational thought and any sense of logic. The holiday cheer was gone, and the negativity was taking chunks out of my butt—not just nipping it. I turned to my niece and said loudly, "No, you will sit where I tell you, and that is the end of it."

I never yell at my niece. She is the best behaved out of the five kids, and the sweetest little girl. She looked up at me with tears in her eyes and just started crying. My sister runs out and says, "What is going on?" I snap at my sister and tell her, "I have had it. Nothing I do is right, and she can sit where I tell her to sit!" Surprisingly, Kara is not mad. She actually seems to be getting enjoyment out of me losing it. She knew what had happened. After all, she was the one who sent me into the kitchen to get dinner moving. She knew the potential consequences.

Kara tried to talk me down, but I was long gone. I was past the point of being rational. My niece was still sobbing and looking at me as if I had stolen Christmas from her.

I stormed into the living room and announced to anyone who would listen, "I have had enough. The kids have worn me out."

Gary, my husband, responds with, "Kids? I've had them all by myself out here for the last hour."

My face must have spoken a thousand words. I didn't care if he had been with the kids most of the time. My perception was that I was dealing with dinner, and the few interruptions from the kids were unacceptable. I was not thinking clearly.

The negativity was now chomping at my thighs. I was ready to explode, even though it was not rational. And then, wham, one sentence from my brother-in-law snapped me out of the negative world and brought me back to reality.

He said to Gary, "Dude, that was not the right thing to say."

I started laughing and thought, *What just happened? How did I let myself get spun up so badly?* It was at that moment that I recognized "it" was a combination of the noise, excitement, my mom's stress and the kids' interruptions. It all came together to create a perfect storm.

I immediately went and found my niece. She would not even look at me. Boy, did I feel like a heel. I sat down next to her and told her I was sorry. Just like most small children do, she accepted my apology immediately, forgot about the incident, and we were buddies once again for the rest of the evening.

Over the next few hours, we had a terrific time eating

dinner, opening presents, decorating cookies for Santa, and then making the special reindeer food (glitter and oats). My sister and I laugh about that incident quite often. I'm sure one of us will have another holiday meltdown at some point because we all know how trying family gatherings can be. But next time, we'll be more aware of what's happening, and at least we wont get nipped so hard.

❀ ❀ ❀ ❀ ❀ ❀

The most beneficial response in this type of situation is to use the "nip" as a learning opportunity. Having negativity nip you in the butt helps you understand what your negative moments feel like. That awareness will help you avoid future negative interactions. In the best cases, being nipped by negativity may even give you a good laugh afterwards, when you come out of your funk.

Kris thinks about that day and how fast she lost her holiday cheer. She feels ashamed she made her niece cry, but she doesn't dwell on it. Everyone will have moments like this, and the best thing to do is to learn from them. Next Christmas Eve she will make sure her negative vibe indicators are fine-tuned, and she'll take precautions to not allow negativity to get her stockings.

Sometimes it's not even other people who can create a negative moment, it's just the situation, or even one's beloved dogs. In the next story, Jeanie recounts her not so positive experience camping with her boys.

Doggone Camping Trip

By Jeanie

Kris and a group of coworkers went camping every year, and they always returned with many fun stories to share about their adventures. Over the years, I became good friends with these folks, and one summer they invited me to join them. My first adventure with this gang was planned for Tobemory, located on the beautiful Bruce Peninsula in Canada.

I was excited about the trip and decided it could be fun to bring my two dogs along, Chance and Ditto. Ditto got his name because he looked remarkably like Chance, even though they weren't even the same mixes of mutts. Chance got his name because we said that we were his last chance when we adopted him from the Society for the Prevention of Cruelty to Animals (SPCA). In hindsight, I doubt we were his last chance, as he was such a sweet dog I am certain he would have been adopted.

Packing the car for a camping trip with two dogs went as smoothly as possible. That was due to my planning. I didn't think I would fit all the stuff and the dogs in the car, so I bought a new cargo carrier. That gave me plenty of room to bring what I needed and freed up lots of space in the car for the dogs to spread out and relax. Every mile into the trip I became more excited about spending a long weekend with fabulous friends. I was hoping this would be the first of many exciting adventures.

Not far into the drive came the first indication that maybe this trip wouldn't live up to my expectations. There was an odd smell coming from the back of my car. I was driving right behind Kris and Gary, so I called Kris on the radio (before cell phones were common, we used two-way radios to communicate while camping) and told her that we needed to pull over. Sure enough, Ditto had thrown up in the back of the car. Luckily, with all my camping supplies I had plenty of stuff to clean it up, and we were on our way again.

About an hour further into the drive, Chance got up and was desperate to get out of the car. He obviously had to go the bathroom. I made another radio call and we made a brief stop again. I was still excited about the trip but at this point, I started wondering if the dogs were going to impact my camping experience. Little did I know, the answer was a resounding yes!

The rest of the drive was uneventful, and setting up my campsite went quick with some help from others in our group. My next priority was fixing dinner for the boys (Chance and Ditto). Dogs are similar to young kids when it comes to eating. They eat on a regular schedule, and they don't like it much when you alter their schedule.

After I placed their bowls of food on the ground, I turned my back to go start my dinner, and they immediately got into a fight. I was able to pull them apart with no damage done to each other; their barks were much worse than their bites. That was the first time they had ever gotten into a fight. These dogs had been living in my home together for years. They were normally the best of buddies. I think the uncertainty of the outdoors and a new environment created some fear in Ditto, which caused him to get aggressive about his food. He was probably just as surprised by his reaction as I was.

I was a little rattled, but the problem was easily solved. For the remainder of the trip, I would separate the two of them while they ate.

After dinner, we joined the gang and had an enjoyable night by the bonfire. Many marshmallows were roasted, s'mores eaten, and laughs shared by all. I remember thinking that life doesn't get much better than being surrounded by good friends. The dogs were so relaxed at my feet that I had practically forgotten about the dinner incident and the minor travel interruptions. My positivity meter was completely full.

Finally, it was time to hit the sack and get some sleep after a great evening. Unfortunately, it was unusually hot during that trip. In my opinion, there is little worse on a camping trip than trying to sleep in the heat. It was made doubly miserable by being trapped in a two-man tent with two sixty-pound, panting dogs. There was no sleep to be had for any of us in that tent.

When I "woke" up in the morning, my positivity level was at most half full. It is extremely hard to maintain a positive attitude with little to no sleep. On top of that, the next day was extremely hot. I am not a fan of hot weather. I prefer a sunny, brisk fall day, where the sun is shining and you can wear a sweater. To make matters worse, throughout the day, it quickly became apparent that the dogs were going to limit my participation with others during the trip.

First, one of the families had their dog with them also, and Ditto wasn't exceptionally friendly with that dog, so hanging out together involved keeping the dogs separated. That wasn't terribly conducive for me to hang out with that family.

I tried hiking with the dogs and some of the group.

It didn't go too smooth. Keep in mind that I was walking with two dogs on leashes. If one of them saw something and darted out, I was being yanked, or their leashes were getting tangled. It was comical for others to watch me spin in multiple directions while I tried to untangle it all. From my perspective, moment by moment the positivity was draining out of me. I was a perfect target for negativity to nip me in the butt.

The campground had a beautiful lake-front beach that made for great snorkeling and swimming. I tried tying the dogs up to a nearby tree so I could enjoy the water activities. But the minute I walked away from them, they started to bark and cry. As long as someone held the leash, they would be quiet. Maybe they were afraid we would leave them tied to a tree and not come back for them. Either way, I did not get to enjoy the water fun.

Every move I made had to be coordinated with another person from the group. That included when I needed to go to the bathroom. Someone else had to watch the dogs so they wouldn't bark and cry. This trip didn't feel relaxing to me and negativity was oozing from my every thought.

Overall, day one did not go well at all or at least live up to my expectations. I was tired, frustrated, and knew I was not winning the nipping the negativity battle. I even felt myself barking at the dogs (figuratively, of course). As I sat by the bonfire that second night, I recognized I was only focusing on the negative. I felt moody and didn't feel like talking to my friends. This was the trip I was so excited about, and here I was with terrific people, sulking and feeling sorry for myself.

To continue to add to my misery, it was unseasonably hot the remainder of the trip. Me and the dogs didn't get very much sleep at all. Each day, I was stuck at the campsite, anchored by two dogs, with little sleep. It was quite stressful and frustrating. All I could think of was *When is this going to end?* I regretted coming on the trip and I felt the negativity cloud over my head. I was not nipping "it" at all. I recognized I needed to do something about it, but I felt powerless to turn the situation around. My friends were trying to help, but my negative dive had gone too deep. I tried to continue with the trip as long as I could, but I was so negative that I couldn't find joy in any part of the vacation. I ended up leaving early to go home with the dogs.

Overall, it may not have been my favorite camping trip, but there were a few pleasant memories, and plenty of lessons to be learned. This same group of friends and I have shared many subsequent trips together, just minus the dogs!

❀ ❀ ❀ ❀ ❀ ❀

As Jeanie showed us in this story, sometimes you just cannot change a situation. She was on her trip with the dogs, during a heat wave in Canada. Negative feelings turned her positive expectations into a lousy time. Once she recognized how she was being affected by the negativity, she chose to remove herself from the situation.

It would be easy to avoid the possibility of negative situations by never investing in our friends, relationships, and life experiences. You're less likely to have negative experiences if you limit your interactions with others. While this may work in the short term, your life will be richer if you put yourself out there and learn to deal effectively with negativity. In the following story, Jeanie talks about putting herself out there and then literally getting "nipped," but upon reflection sees that sometimes life is worth that nip.

Bonds and Bites

By Jeanie

Years ago, in Western New York, I used to host game nights at my house, where friends would come over and we would play board games. It was always a good opportunity for a few laughs and some quiet fun together.

After a game night one October evening, as everyone was left, a bottle of wine was accidentally dropped on the driveway and broke. I grabbed a push broom from the backyard to sweep up the glass, but in my focus on the glass, I forgot to shut the gate.

Later that night, I let out my dogs Chance, Ditto, and Webster. Within minutes I remembered the gate. I ran out and I found no dogs in the backyard. My heart dropped. I walked out the gate, and there stood Webster in the neighbor's yard. Since he was basking in his new-found freedom, he wouldn't come to me. I ran back in the house and grabbed a slice of cheese. I went back outside, showed Webster the cheese, and he came right back into the yard. It's like those old commercials used to say, "Ah, the power of cheese."

Still, Chance and Ditto were nowhere to be found. I jumped in the car with no coat on and started driving around the neighborhood, frantically looking for them. I was driving with the window down, yelling their names, but I had no luck finding them. I saw the neighbors, and they offered to help look for the dogs. It was getting dark, and I lived in a neighborhood near Niagara Falls Boulevard, which is an exceptionally busy four-lane road. And I was worried they would make their way out to that road. Now I was beginning to panic.

Driving around with the car window down and no coat on caused me to become extremely cold. I decided to stop at the house and grab my coat. I ran in, grabbed my coat, and raced back outside to resume my search. On my way out of the house, I looked up and there Chance and Ditto were walking up the driveway, as if they had been out for an evening stroll.

That night changed my life. Since that incident, anytime I see a stray dog, I stop to try to help the dog return home. I know how upset and worried I was that Chance and Ditto would get hurt when they were missing. It was scary. I don't want any dog owner to feel the way I did.

Over time, I have had the opportunity to help many strays. One quite funny rescue involved a Bassett Hound with no identification that I found in my neighborhood. I got him to get in my car and then I drove him around the nearby neighborhoods to see if anyone recognized him. Every time I got out of the car to ask someone about him, the Bassett Hound jumped in the front seat and honked the horn! That was quite an adventure. But it turned out well because we quickly found his grateful owner.

On another day, I was heading to work when I saw a stray dog on the sidewalk of my street. I went back to the house to get a dog biscuit, hoping to persuade him to come closer so I could get him in the car. He came to me when I offered the biscuit, and I reached around and grabbed his collar. What a mistake that was! He totally panicked and ended up biting me in several spots on my right hand and arm. He did not bite me out of aggression, but out of fear. I spent the rest of that day in the emergency room, and the next several weeks getting rabies shots. As I sat in the emergency room, waiting to be treated, I thought about how bad the situation was. I should have known better than to try to grab a stray dog. It was a painful lesson. At the time, I was feeling pretty negative and thinking I may never try to help a stray again.

So, you might be thinking that experience cured me of trying to catch strays. Well, not really. After I had some time to reflect, I realized that although it was a negative experience, I couldn't let it change who I am fundamentally. I couldn't let it wipe out all the joy that I had been able to bring to others by returning their beloved pets. And I couldn't allow it to erase my joy at saving the lives of stray animals.

I often think that this situation is similar to those involving humans. In our lives, we sometimes have negative experiences, or meet people who disappoint us, or even hurt us, but we can't let that stop us from living life to its fullest. There is a certain amount of risk when we open ourselves up to new people and new situations. Sometimes they will not meet our expectations. By opening up to all possibilities we may be disappointed, but more times than not we will be rewarded. We will be rewarded externally by meeting extraordinary people who enrich our lives. And we will be rewarded internally through the joy that comes from close and lasting friendships. The loving bonds and satisfaction we feel will far outweigh the occasional bite.

How you react in a situation usually determines how you

will feel when it is over. Will you feel drained and be negative, or more uplifted and positive? In all cases, you have the power to recognize the moments and influence the outcomes.

In Jeanie's story, getting bitten by the dog could have made her feel upset, frustrated, or angry. It could have caused her to quit saving dogs altogether. But that's not what happened. She chose to view the incident as a random event and not let it change her optimistic attitude for saving strays.

Staying in a negative moment without nipping it in the butt or flipping the tables, will not make you feel happy. It will bring you down emotionally and most likely physically. However, that experience can actually become a motivator. Use it to work harder to get out of the negative moment by nipping, it, rather than being nipped. Now that we have shown you what "it" is and some specific examples of recognizing "it," the remainder of this book will walk you through some techniques to help you start nipping and flipping!

Chapter 3

Pause
It

Stop, Breathe, and Assess the Situation

Every second of every day can be positive or negative. It's easy to get caught up in the negativity or the downward spiral of a moment. And it takes more energy to keep a positive outlook when those around you are being negative. However, when you do take the high road, you will feel better. Negative energy drains people and brings them down. Positive energy uplifts people and gives them more energy to move forward. It's your choice; you have the ability to stop negativity in its tracks and "nip it in the butt!"

As mentioned in the previous chapters, you first have to become aware of and recognize the moment. Next,-fine-tune those negative vibe indicators. That will take some practice, but you'll soon master it. Once you recognize the moment, we recommend that you pause. One simple way to pause is to stop and focus on your breathing. Take a few deep breaths. Then, if needed, stop and briefly analyze the entire situation to understand what is going on before speaking or acting.

Pausing can be more challenging than you may think. When a negative situation is staring us in the face—especially one filled with chaos— it's sometimes difficult to stop ourselves from immediately reacting. However, by stopping for a few seconds, we give ourselves crucial time to alter our thoughts and then control how a situation will progress.

While you are pausing, use those precious seconds to let your initial reaction pass and regain composure and calmness. Then you will be able to think more clearly and logically, with less emotion about a situation. After this pause, you will be ready to ACT, rather than REact to a situation. Following this approach will give you more control over the outcome.

As you will see from some of our personal stories throughout this book, when we find ourselves in a moment that feels like we are ready to yell, curse, or maybe even throw something, we try to just pause for a moment. Most of the time we stop, breathe, and think about what's happening. We think about what's causing the situation and the impact it has on us. And most importantly, we think about the affect our words will have on the situation.

In this chapter, we will illustrate how you can begin to recognize the negativity of a situation and pause to help control your reaction. By choosing how you react to a situation, you will "nip negativity in the butt" and "flip the tables" of the moment. Our next story shows how Gary used a deep breath to give himself time to react positively to a negative situation.

The Ruptured Hose

By Kris

A neighbor asked my husband Gary if he would assist with replacing a hydraulic hose on her tractor. She had previously tried doing it herself, but couldn't get it on tight enough. Gary agreed, and he even made room in our heated garage so they could work in a warm space. After about thirty minutes, and with everything going relatively smoothly, they were all done replacing the hose. Gary suggested testing everything just to make sure the blade was working properly. As she lowered the blade, a different hose burst and oil started gushing all over the clean garage floor.

Now, you can imagine, this took them both by surprise. One minute they were relaxed, thinking they were done with the project, and the next second there was oil spewing at them from a different part of the tractor. In hindsight, the scene sounds comical, but at the time, it sure wasn't very funny to either of them.

Our neighbor started muttering some expletives and apologized for making a mess. Gary was thinking the same thoughts, but he recognized that she was upset and was creating a spiral of energy that could have pulled them both down. She wasn't doing this because she is a negative person. In reality, she is a tremendously positive person who is a joy to be around, but the moment overtook her and she got caught up in the negativity. Gary, who was feeling her energy and was a bit overwhelmed with the oil that was continuing to spill, quickly assessed the situation and decided not to add fuel to the fire. He told me that although it was hard to do, he took a deep breath and told her, "No big deal. It could have been worse. Better this happened now rather than in the middle of a snowstorm."

Instantly the mood in the garage improved. His words lifted the spirits of our neighbor and prevented him from falling into the negative spiral with her. She appreciated what he said, and her only words were "thank you." They were then both able to smile about it, but at that point they weren't quite ready to laugh.

Gary disconnected the hose that controlled the blade, and our neighbor drove the tractor home. The next week when she received the new hose, she came over and they connected it. Everything worked perfectly! Now they were ready to laugh about the whole incident!

❀ ❀ ❀ ❀ ❀ ❀

Here was a situation that was truly at a fork in the road. The words that were to come out of Gary's mouth were the deciding factor in how it would progress. Based on his response, Gary and his neighbor were both able to "flip the tables" of the energy of the moment. Neither of them could change the fact that there was a broken hose without a replacement. What they could change was how they reacted to the situation. That part was entirely in their power.

It genuinely does help to take a deep breath, assess the situation, and think about what you will say. How can you practice this skill? Start by taking deep breaths throughout your day. While you are sitting at your desk, taking a break at work, watching television, or cooking dinner, just stop for a few seconds and take some deep breaths. Get in the habit of pulling in full, deep breaths of fresh air. Think about the air coming in and going out. Relax your mind. Let your stress go when you breathe out.

Once you have mastered taking a deep breath when you are alone, practice pausing with everyone you talk to. Count to two or three before responding. This will help you practice pausing in non emotional situations, so it can become a habit. Then, when you find yourself in a negative, emotional situation, you will be pausing naturally.

As you become more comfortable with pausing, start assessing the situations you are in during that pause. Try to understand how the other person is feeling. Formulate a potential response by anticipating their reaction to the situation. That's a lot to do in a few seconds, when the moment is positive. When negativity is introduced, it becomes much harder to stop and think.

In our immediate reaction to a situation, emotions run high, and too often we speak out of that emotion rather than from thoughtful contemplation. It's recommended that you practice pausing and assessing in everyday situations, even when emotion is not involved. The more you practice, the more natural it will become.

You'll find yourself taking a minor pause in every situation, and truly thinking about your words before you speak. More importantly, you will start to understand how your words will impact the situation. You'll begin to recognize how negative words increase the downward spiral of a negative moment. Likewise, positive words help douse the fire of a negative moment and bring peace to it. Which outcome would you rather have in your life? In the next story, Jeanie pauses for a minute to take a few breaths, and that enables her to diffuse a highly emotional situation that many of us have faced.

The Car Accident

By Jeanie

I was driving in Frederick, Maryland, on my way to a Hero Dogs event. Frederick has a lot of one-way streets. I was concentrating on my GPS, which was not giving instructions fast enough for the close quarters of the city, so I was focused on "looking" at the GPS screen. Big mistake!

I was in the right lane and I saw on the screen that I needed to make a left-hand turn. I forgot for a split second that I was on a one-way street, and to my left there was another lane of traffic going in the same direction I was. I started to make the left turn and hit another vehicle. The vehicle kept moving forward and almost totally ripped off my front bumper.

I, along with the driver of the other car, pulled over to the side of the road. There were three women in the other car. They jumped out and I asked if they were hurt. They said "no", but they were emotional and very angry. The driver of the car immediately started looking for witnesses so she could prove that the accident was not her fault. I was shaken and my emotions were running high as well, but I took a minute to breathe. I thought, "Okay, no one is hurt and cars can be fixed. This is not that big a deal."

After pausing for a moment, I told the other driver,

"You don't need a witness. I was at fault. I turned in front of you." Those few statements immediately diffused the situation. The police came and I told the officer the same thing.

A nice man, who lived on the street, used his multi-tool to remove my bumper that was now hanging off my car. I threw the bumper into the trunk and went on to the event. I was a little late, but it all turned out well. By pausing, I was able to turn a potentially emotional and negative situation into a neutral one. None of us wanted our cars damaged, but I think given the circumstances, the situation turned out okay for all of us, except for my insurance company, which wasn't very happy that I admitted I was at fault.

In Jeanie's story, even though there were longer-term consequences of what she said, Jeanie tried to diffuse a potentially negative situation by reassuring the other driver that everything would be alright. She paused and considered how the first things she said were going to influence the other driver's reaction. Considering the consequences and effects of our words is a skill we learn as we mature, but sometimes we need to pause to use those skills.

As small children, we say the first thing that pops into our minds, since we have not yet learned to consider the consequences of our words. We are taught that we should consider the feelings of others before we speak. We are told to ask ourselves "How will that make the other person feel? Will it offend them or make them feel uncomfortable?" The more we practice that skill of considering others, the better we get at it. This holds true especially regarding negative situations. In these cases, think about how your words will impact the energy of the moment and the other people involved.

When there is a potentially negative situation staring you in the face, it may feel easier to join in the negativity rather than be positive. But what good will that do? Normally, it just makes everyone in the situation feel worse and leads to a downward spiral. Instead, stop for a moment to pause, think about your words, and then act. Dig deep if you have to, but find some positive words or positive thoughts. It may be hard, and sometimes some negativity may still slip out.

We have all been in a situation where time stands still for a second and tempers could flare. We're referring to a situation where everyone involved feels the stress, anger, or frustration. We have all experienced those times in which we know people are stressed, and what comes out of our mouths could be the straw that breaks the camel's back, or the words of peace that diffuse the situation. How we react in those moments can truly define the outcome of the situation.

We can think logically about "nipping negativity in the butt." On paper, it seems so easy to alter our behavior and change our words in negative situations. Sometimes, though, our emotions get the best of us. The following story has two examples of how that initial emotion can cause us to speak before we take a moment to pause. Even the most positive people can have these moments. But being aware of how we are feeling (our "negative vibe indicators"), and how others are feeling, can help change our actions quickly and turn a negative situation into one that's more positive.

Yogurt and Syrup

By Kris

If you have young kids and understand how hectic meal time can be, feel free to skip a few paragraphs. I need to use the next few paragraphs to set the stage before the actual yogurt incident, so you understand my frame of mind. After a long commute home from work that involved picking up two kids from different places, I finally arrived home with both of my hungry and tired little munchkins. For some reason, the magic food fairy did not stop at our house that day and have dinner ready for us, so I had to whip up some dinner.

I always hope that since the kids don't see each other all day, maybe when we get home they will play nicely and quietly, and enjoy each other's company. That would give me a few moments of peace to make dinner. But no, it's always quite opposite. And on that particular day, in between the little ones' constant bickering, I was rewarded with a number of their visits to the kitchen. They didn't hesitate to tell me just what was on their minds.

"I don't want chicken for dinner."

"I do not like peas."

"Mom, how about having pizza for dinner?"

"Is dinner done? I am REALLY hungry."

"Mom, why does it take so long to make dinner?

"Mommy—I am REALLY, REALLY hungry!"

"Mommy, Matthew hit me."

"I only did that because Sara threw a Lego at me."

"Mom, I am as hungry as a horse."

And so it went on like this for ten more minutes.

Gary came home from work right as I was setting the table. I was trying to quicken my pace because I knew I had a ticking time bomb on my hands. When the kids get overly hungry, they have meltdowns. I did not feel like dealing with one of those. So I decided the smart thing to do was to carry more on each trip to the table. That didn't work out so well.

Two open yogurt containers slipped out of my hands. It was as if everything went into slow motion at that moment. I saw the containers slowly drop and hit the floor. Then, time sped up as I was hit in the face and front of my body with strawberry yogurt. I figured I got the worst of it. As I surveyed the kitchen, it looked like a gallon of yogurt had exploded. Who knew two small jars of yogurt could cause so much damage?

I just stood there in disbelief. I took some deep breaths to keep myself calm… until Gary decided to chime in a bit.

"Why were you carrying so much? This is a mess!"

"Really? A mess? Gee, I didn't notice!" I thought the sarcasm in my voice would give him a warning, but he just couldn't stop.

"How could you drop two containers of yogurt?"

I contemplated picking up a container and demonstrating how I dropped it, but I figured that was a crummy idea and could only lead to a worse outcome. Instead, I looked at him and said, calmly, "There is nothing you can say that will make me feel any worse than I feel right now."

In essence, I was asking him to take a deep breath and carefully think about his next words. And it worked remarkably well, because his response was, "Can you hand me some towels? I will clean it up."

So now, fast forward one month. We were in the kitchen with my dear friend, Paula, cooking breakfast. Paula was cutting fruit and I was making pancakes. Gary was between Paula and me at the sink, wiping syrup off the outside of the syrup container. Just a few minutes prior, I had refilled the container with fresh maple syrup and must have dripped some syrup. While Gary was wiping the container, he removed the top. All of a sudden I hear Gary yell, "Oh, no!"

Right at that moment, time slowed down again. It was déjà vous. I watched the bottle slip from his hand and hit the floor. As soon as the bottle hit, time sped up. The syrup flew into the air and landed all over Gary's jeans, Paula's pants, the cupboards, and the floor. It was a mess. I was the first to speak (without even thinking or pausing). "How did you drop it?"

As soon as the words came out of my mouth, I knew they were wrong. My head wanted to keep going, but my heart knew nothing I could say would make him feel any worse. So, I tried to recover. "No big deal, it will clean up easily."

Gary grunted softly and grabbed some clean towels for both of us. He quietly muttered noises the whole time we were cleaning up the mess. I knew he was frustrated. He kept his composure, though, by taking deep breaths. I could actually hear his exhales. Later, he told me that since he couldn't find nice words to say in the moment, he remained quiet. He told me in his heart he knew that although it was a giant mess, in the grand scheme of life it just didn't matter.

❀ ❀ ❀ ❀ ❀ ❀

When you are in the moment, and something like flying syrup is literally in your face, sometimes your initial reaction is to speak without thinking about the consequences. Try to remember that you have the power to instantly change that moment for yourself or someone else.

Kris' yoga instructor once talked about the importance of listening to your body and staying focused. She said subtle movement changes will change the way each pose feels. Similarly, there are so many moments in life, and each moment can be completely different, depending on your state of mind and your actions. She likened it to going out in a blizzard with an unzipped jacket on. The simple act of zipping up the jacket will change the moment for you dramatically.

Taking a second to pause can change the feeling of the moment in a profound way. Pausing may stop your initial thoughts from becoming actual words you may regret. Mastering the pause is the key to successfully flipping the tables of a negative situation into a positive one.

It is up to you. Do you want to "nip negativity in the butt"? Do you want a happier life? If so, then moment by moment find ways to add positivity.

Stop and pause before you say anything.

And don't beat yourself up if once in a while those negative thoughts come flying out of your mouth as words. It's going to happen. When it does, hopefully you'll recognize what you're doing in relation to that particular situation. Are you adding positivity or negativity?

When you do find a way to be positive in the moment, your moments will turn into minutes, and those minutes into hours. Before you know it, your days will seem more positive, and you'll find yourself smiling more. Ideally those around you will take notice, you'll find all your relationships and interactions with people have shifted, and everything just feels better. What a fabulous life it is!

Chapter 4

Spin It

View Negativity from a Different Angle

You are in control of your perspective in every moment you face. It's true. Is your glass half empty or is your glass always half full? Similar to the popular saying "There are two sides to every story," we propose "There are two ways to look at every moment." When you are in a negative situation, the perspective you choose is entirely under your control and can make the difference in how you will ultimately feel about the immediate moment.

For example, if you get stuck at a traffic light for

longer than you expect, how do you react? Do you view it is a nuisance and get grumpy or do you view it as a normal occurrence in life and not even waste another second worrying about it?

If someone cuts you off on the highway, do you view it as a direct insult to you and feel road rage creeping into your pores or do you view it simply as someone being a bit careless and ease off the gas and give them space?

In each situation, you choose your reaction based on the way you perceive the moment. When you change your perception, or 'spective as we like to say, your reaction will change as well. More peaceful reactions to potentially negative situations will bring more peace into your life. Try this approach, and you'll begin to see more positivity in every moment.

One day in Yoga class, Kris' instructor presented the following story and asked the class which "blade" they were.

> *Imagine yourself sitting in a grassy field on a sunny, warm day. It is slightly breezy, and you begin to focus your attention on a few blades of grass. One blade is flowing with the wind, bending and straightening as it needs to. The other blade of grass stands tall and fights the wind. It wiggles a little as it goes against the wind, but for the most part, it stands tall and does not budge. As you focus on those blades, which blade resonates with you? The one that's moving with ease, or the one that's resisting the wind?*

While you read the stories in this chapter, think about which blade of grass you are. Do you go with the flow, or are you stubborn in your moments? If you tend to go with the flow, you are more likely viewing your moments from different perspectives. If you tend to be the blade of grass that doesn't move with the wind, you most likely view the negative moments as negative and don't try to see them from a different angle. Which blade do you think feels more peaceful with its life?

Sometimes when we're feeling particularly negative and rigid in our viewpoint, it takes someone else to help us see another perspective. In the next story, Kris' children helped her to go with the flow and turn a potentially bad day into a great day.

A Snowy Day

By Kris

It was the winter of 2010. We had received an early dump of snow and hadn't seen grass in eight weeks. I live in Western New York, so this is a common occurrence. For the most part, we Western New Yorkers are a hardy crew and accept the weather. We choose to live here, and we embrace all four incredible seasons—from 90 degrees hot and muggy, to the cold, dreary days of winter.

On this particular day, it was overcast with light snow, but not too cold. My son and daughter were playing in the backyard while I watched them from the warm kitchen, catching up on Facebook. A friend of mine from high school had posted how delightful it was where he lived, "Sunny, 70 degrees, and blue skies. Nowhere on Earth would I rather be."

I immediately started having negative thoughts like, *This darn weather. Are you kidding me? Where is spring?* I began feeling sorry that I was dealing with overcast skies and snow. When I start to feel sorry for myself, my whole attitude changes, and I can feel the negativity seep in every pore. I get grumpy, my shoulders tighten, and there's a knot in the pit of my stomach. As I write this, I can't imagine ever choosing to bring in that energy, but we all do at one time or another. After all, we are human and can't be positive with our thoughts all the time. The key in changing your life, though, is to recognize when you are in a negative mode and to pay attention to how your body feels.

On this particular snowy day, I didn't even recognize what was happening to me until I looked outside and an altogether different feeling overtook me. I was smiling, and my posture became straighter. Instead of a knot in my stomach, I could feel a giggle building. What caused this?

It was as simple as seeing one of my children happily making angels in the snow over and over again. He was making multiple angels, forming a full circle of them holding hands. My other child was running around and catching snowflakes on her tongue. They were both living in the moment and enjoying what Mother Nature was dishing out. Nothing would have persuaded them to be anywhere else but in the snow in our backyard at that moment.

I got up from the table, closed my laptop, and put on my snow clothes. I spent the next hour with my kids, making snow angels and catching snowflakes on my tongue. We ended our snow time with a very long snowball fight. There is no way you will ever outsmart Mother Nature. In situations like this, the only way to enjoy her is to join her! At that moment, there was no place I rather would have been. I was so appreciative to my kids for showing me a different 'spective of the moment.

Whether negative thoughts creep up on you subconsciously or whether you consciously decide to be negative, these thoughts carry some physical side effects with them. You can choose to let these feelings go. When you decide to take the positive route, you

will notice a difference emotionally, physically, and spiritually. As you start to sense you are going into a negative moment, take that pause and think about what's causing it. Look around and see how others are responding. In the previous story, the kids were having a marvelous time. Kris' attitude changed when she took her cue from the kids. They showed her how to make the most of what was in front of her. What a happy way to live life!

Sometimes we can help other people look at the situation from a different angle. They may not understand it or be able to see it fully, but they may stop being negative, if for a moment. In the following story, some names have been changed, but the premise is accurate. Many times people do not even realize they are being negative. They may just need a gentle reminder to look at the situation from a new angle.

Fred

By Kris

We all have a Fred in our life. You know who he is. He's the guy who is nice on the surface. He smiles. He talks to you at the water cooler or at the kids' baseball game. He's always willing to help out. You can count on him to get the job done, volunteer for the committee, and pick up the donuts for the morning meeting. The list goes on and on.

Most people seem to like him, but… there is just something about him that makes you not want to spend a lot of time with him. How can that be? He seems nice, helps when needed, and is dependable. There is just something, something that's hard to put your finger on. Let's look a little deeper at Fred and see what's really going on.

Fred talks to everyone, smiles, and seems generally pleasant. But when you analyze his conversations, there is something more there. That something is actually a negative undertone. Here are a few snippets from Fred's conversations with different people:

"Hi, Delores. How are you? Doing great here, if it just weren't for the weather. I am so sick and tired of the rain. Why can't we get some more sun?"

"Hey, Caleb. Thanks for letting me help out on the

charity committee. It's a great cause, but you know I think we should find a better way to select the charity next year. I just don't get the feeling that any thought was put into it."

"Hi, Frank. How are you? Sorry I didn't get a chance to chat with you at the kids' baseball game last night. They played hard and they sure had fun. But that umpire was something else. Where did they get him anyway? Could you believe those calls? I thought he was just lousy."

"Hi, Melinda. Nice job on your presentation yesterday. Did you see Roger got that promotion? Do you honestly think he deserves it? After all, he's only been here two years. I wonder if management even considered others."

Fred starts out happy and pleasant, however, there is always a "but." He can't let a positive moment or thought stay positive. He follows up each positive statement with something negative. Think of how exhausting that must be for the listener. In each case, the listener is engaging in what appears to be an upbeat conversation. Then the listener immediately gets hit with a negative statement. A Fred personality can definitely drain someone's energy.

Let's review this conversation with Melinda. I'm going to present two different approaches Melinda could have used to respond to Fred. Choose which one would you rather be a part of.

"Thanks, Fred. I truly appreciate the feedback about my presentation. And yes, I did hear about Roger. I cannot believe it. He did not deserve it as much as Katrina or even Jacqueline. He just got it because the boss likes him. I don't know what they were thinking."

With that approach, both Melinda and Fred may walk away feeling bitter or angry. What if Melinda responded to Fred in the following way?

"Thanks, Fred. I truly appreciate the feedback about my presentation. I worked really hard on it, and I think the customer was impressed, too. I did hear about Roger. Great for him! I'm sure the boss must have felt he was the best fit for the job and will help the company move forward. I'm really looking forward to working with him in the future."

In the second approach, Melinda does a terrific job of funneling a potentially negative situation into a much more upbeat one. She can walk away from the conversation feeling happy and excited about working with Roger in his new role. This approach may ultimately change the way Fred views the situation as well.

This example shows us that each and every moment in our lives will result in us feeling a certain way. We can either feel positive and full of energy, or negative and totally drained. Which would you rather feel? When you feel the latter, with your energy slipping away, think about what you can do to "nip negativity in the butt" and "flip the tables" of the moment. When you take charge of the situation, you will walk away feeling better.

In the next story, Jeanie's friend, Walter, could choose to get "stuck" and allow anger or resentment to pull him down emotionally. Instead, he turned his frustration around and propelled himself forward and became energized. He was able to turn a negative into a positive.

Walter's Story

By Jeanie

Let's talk about the relationships we have with people who bring us down, and how we can find ways to change so that they do not have such a negative impact on us. Allow me to explain further by telling you a story about Walter.

Extremely competent at his job, Walter struggled to please his boss. According to Walter, he could never do enough to make his boss happy. Every time he prepared a presentation, his boss criticized the content, the format, the order, and just about everything else. Walter used to spend hours working on a presentation, but no matter how long he worked on it, the presentation was criticized. Several times, Walter's boss viewed the presentation on a screen so he could review it with Walter. The first thing his boss did was put the presentation in edit mode, even before he looked at it!

It got to the point where Walter would think, *Why bother?" I can spend ten hours or two hours on this, and either way it won't be good enough, so why should I waste my time?* The real kicker was that Walter's boss had good ideas, and many of his suggested changes did improve the presentations. However, Walter saw this as the difference between great and good enough. He was frustrated because he felt that many of the presentations he worked on were not critical to the company and would only be given once. The entire situation was making Walter miserable.

Walter's boss was hurting Walter's self-esteem and causing him to feel indifferent. He started to just throw the presentations together at the last minute and then let his boss edit them. This approach did not make Walter feel any better. He had always been a top performer, and doing substandard work didn't sit well with him. Yet, he felt that his boss had unrealistic standards of perfection on each and every assignment. From Walter's viewpoint, that perfection, and the associated time and effort, should have been reserved for the most significant presentations or other assignments.

Have you ever been in a situation like Walter's? Sometimes people in our lives put unrealistic expectations on us, and we struggle to live up to those expectations. And when we can't live up to them, we feel as though we have failed. We feel inadequate about ourselves, and it can seriously impact our relationships with those people.

What do you think Walter should have done in this situation? He truly had a chance to "nip it in the butt." He had the power to rethink how he handled the situation and stop this constant criticism. The most important thing he could have done was change his thinking about his boss. His boss probably wasn't thinking, *I'm criticizing Walter.* He was more likely thinking, *I'm making sure the presentation is the best it can be.*

Do you see the difference in these two statements? The first sentence is negative, the second positive. The boss believed he was doing something positive, so Walter might have thought about perceiving it that way. Even if Walter changed his perspective, repeated criticism can wear down the most enthusiastic employee. So another way that Walter might have handled the situation was to tell his boss how he felt and how the constant criticism was affecting him. After a conversation like that, his boss may have perceived the situation differently and understood perfection is not always needed.

Another way Walter could have handle the situation was to plan for success. As soon as Walter was given an assignment, he could have planned out his presentation. He could have met with his boss and gone over his plan, letting his boss have input at the beginning before he started any real work on the presentation. It would also helped Walter gain some insight into what his boss was looking for and allow them to discuss options and ideas for the presentation. This approach may have helped stop the criticism before it even started, the essence of "nipping it in the butt."

Walter's story is based on actual events so I know how it turned out for him. First of all, Walter decided to think positively about the situation. The first thing he did was stop calling the comments "criticism" and started calling them "feedback." Sometimes a subtle change in wording can begin to shift your perspective of an entire situation.

Walter then began thinking of the reviews as mentoring sessions. He started jotting down key messages from the feedback he received from his boss. He took those ideas and looked for ways to use them on future presentations. Using his boss' feedback would surely help him meet his expectations on future assignments.

Walter also began having quick brainstorming sessions with his boss when presentations were assigned, to ensure he understood the overriding purpose and expectations. These sessions gave Walter a chance to express his ideas about the presentation and hear his boss' ideas, too.

Wow! Now it honestly felt collaborative. Walter certainly felt he had a clear path on where he wanted to go on each presentation. He also found that when he got the key messages and themes right in his presentation, his boss was less likely to criticize things like format or layout. Ultimately, his boss cared about the content.

Just by changing his way of thinking about the situation and his boss, Walter was able to open himself up to learn from his boss, improve his relationship with his boss through more collaboration, and genuinely become more satisfied in his job every day.

Overall, changing attitudes like this can have a significant impact on one's life. Walter enjoyed work again and was happy about going into the office. Most people spend more hours at work than they do with their families. If this is true of you, strive to be happy at work. It will make your life more satisfying.

Trying to view the moment from the "bigger picture" is a new perspective you can bring to a situation. In Krispective speak, we might say, "Don't get caught up in a forest fire" or "Look for the mountain over the forest" or "See the forest through the trees." In other words, don't get stuck in the moment. Look for that bigger picture, as Jeanie explains this in her next story.

Critical Chris

By Jeanie

Being in the Marines, combined with my love of dogs, makes me a perfect fit for a charity that I am very involved in — Hero Dogs, Inc. The charity's mission is to provide independence and improved quality of life to our nation's veterans by raising, training, and placing service dogs ("Hero Dogs") with injured or disabled military veterans who have served honorably in the United States Armed Forces. And I am honored that I was selected to lead this charity's Development Committee (DevCom).

As a young non-profit run almost entirely by volunteers, there is a certain amount of organized chaos. So when I was assigned to lead the DevCom, I created a businesslike, organized presentation on what we would be doing for the year. When I gave the presentation to the board, everyone seemed pleased, since it was the first time anyone had documented a comprehensive development plan with goals, measures, etc.

A guest in the audience named Chris was applying to be a board member. He began to criticize the way the organization operated, i.e., how funds were raised and volunteers were not trained. My first thought was, *I did all this work putting together this plan, and here he is criticizing it.* I just wanted to say to him, *Hey, this is more than anyone else has ever done, it's the first time we have had a comprehensive plan.* I was not happy with Chris at all, and I could feel the physical signs that I was in a negative moment.

I then took a deep breath, paused, and thought to myself, *We need active board members who care and who are willing to take action to move Hero Dogs forward. While he might not have picked the best time to speak up, he obviously cares, and we need that.* Rather than getting defensive, I decided to say, "Those are great insights, Chris, and some great suggestions for how we can do things better." And I asked him to join the DevCom!

I tried to look beyond the immediate negative encounter and toward a longer-term view of the situation. In the end, Chris turned out to be a terrific addition to the DevCom. I have since learned that this way of communicating is simply his style. Sometimes in a work setting you have to interact with a person for a while before you understand their perspectives. I'm glad that, in the heat of the moment, I didn't say the initial words that came to mind. With my pause, and viewing the moment from a new angle, a long-term view, I was able to turn what I perceived as a negative into something positive, not only for me but for the charity.

❁ ❁ ❁ ❁ ❁ ❁

It's hard to gather your thoughts when you are in a moment that may put you in a defensive mode. But it's worth making the effort to pause and stay positive. In most situations, the outcome will make everyone feel better. And when you reflect on the moment, we bet you'll be glad you chose to stay positive and not engage with negativity. When you engage someone from a positive perspective, it's extremely hard for them not to respond in the same manner.

We mentioned at the beginning of the chapter that there are at least two perspectives to every moment — your perspective and the perspective of the person or people you are sharing the moment with. In the following story, Jeanie has to take action to address another person's perception, even though Jeanie believed it was not reality. Because Jeanie took a moment to understand what the other person was thinking, she learned a skill that she has used throughout her leadership career.

I Am Not a Child

By Jeanie

There once was a woman who worked for me as an editor. She was extremely smart and extraordinarily well read. She was knowledgeable

and experienced, but, required detailed explanations of what needed to be done before she could accomplish an assigned task. So I slowly walked her through each step of what she needed to do. And I thought I was giving her what she wanted: detailed explanations.

Her view of the situation was that I was being condescending, because I would talk to her slowly. She perceived me as talking down to her, and she went to my boss and complained about the way she was being treated. To put it simply, she felt I was treating her like a child.

I was surprised when I got called into my boss' office to discuss the situation. My initial reaction was, *Why did she go to my boss? Why didn't she talk to me? Why did she think I was being condescending? I was just trying to help her.* At that moment, I felt particularly negative about her, my boss, and work.

After talking to my boss and taking some time to cool down, I thought a lot about both sides of our situation. I did not think I was being condescending, but her perception was her reality, so I needed to change something that I was doing. I sat down with her and first apologized for treating her in a way that was condescending. I told her I would make every effort to change, but that she should bring it to my attention should it happen again. I was much more aware of how I spoke to her, and I worked hard to make sure I was treating her with respect.

As I continued to work with that editor, I came to realize that she liked to do exceptional quality work and always meet her customer's expectations. This led her to want detailed explanations, so that she could do her work correctly the first time. So I came to understand her motivations. This awareness helped me become a better leader. Now I look for motivating factors with all employees. This lesson has served me well throughout my career.

❀ ❀ ❀ ❀ ❀ ❀

In Jeanie's story, she immediately was told about the other side of the situation. She knew exactly how the other person perceived it. Jeanie didn't have to guess or make any assumptions. She could take that knowledge and adjust her behavior to help create a more positive environment for both her and the editor.

But what about when you are in a situation with a stranger, where you have no idea regarding their view of the situation. Sometimes it may help if you just cut the person a little slack and try to remain positive. In the following story, Kris was struggling with a stranger until she understood the stranger's perspective of the situation. Once she viewed it from the other side, she changed her reaction.

A Pain in the Nurse

By Kris

I always try to look for the best in someone. When I see negative behavior, I try to understand the root cause of it (that is the engineer in me). For example, most times when a two-year-old is having a temper tantrum, they are not acting out "just because." There is normally a reason for the behavior, whether hunger, fatigue, or the frustration of not being able to express himself or herself. Once you understand the reason, it's usually easier to avoid getting caught up in the temper tantrum and remain patient. Eventually the tantrum ends and everyone goes back to being happy.

Understanding the reason behind a negative outburst with your child, a family member, or a close friend is normally fairly easy because you know their attitudes and personalities. But what do you do when a complete stranger gets under your skin and saps your energy so much it even affects your behavior?

Around the time of this incident, I had experienced a few stressful weeks. My employer went through a round of layoffs and I said goodbye to a lot of friends and people I had worked with for ten or more years. Then, my daughter had surgery to have tubes put in her ears to stop recurring ear infections. Although minor surgery, it's still hard as a mom to watch your little girl being taken away by nurses. You know they're going to put her under, and when she wakes up she will be terrified not knowing what is going on.

On the same evening as my daughter's surgery, my mom was admitted into the hospital with a severe case of pneumonia. The following day, my mom was moved to the cardiac floor to deal with some issues with her heart.

I was trying to balance work, family, and hospital visits, and I slowly felt my positive outlook fading. Adding to all of that, I was worried about my mom. She was getting sicker with each passing day and didn't have her usual fighting spirit. And I definitely was not the normal positive Kris during this time — I was just too darned tired for it.

I was at the hospital one day visiting Mom. Feeling sick, she was extremely uncomfortable. She was complaining that the nurses on the cardiac floor were not as nice as the nurses on the other floor. I dug deep and pulled out some encouraging words to try and not let the conversation turn into a nurse-bashing talk. I tried telling Mom she needed to be tolerant and recognize the patients on this floor were more critical. Perhaps the nurses sometimes had to be quick and that could come across as not being friendly. My mom rolled her eyes at me. Ever since I had been a child, that gesture was her universal sign that she did not agree with me.

As soon as Mom rolled her eyes, nurse Maya walked into the room. She made no eye contact with either my mom or me. She just stared at her computer screen, asked the standard questions, and kept typing. Mom was struggling to hear a few of the questions, so I answered for her. Maya turned to me, and in a stern, condescending voice said, "I am asking her." Now, I may be a positive person, but when some stranger is disrespectful to me, I have an unusually short fuse. She continued in this manner for a few more minutes and I continued to answer for my mom when she couldn't hear. "I am asking her" is what I kept getting from Maya.

It was becoming a power struggle between Maya and me. Who would give in first? I let her suck me right into this volley. I was tired and worried about my mom, and now I had a nurse treating me like a kindergartener. As Maya walked out, I followed her, about ready to explode. I stopped her, and with every ounce of energy I had left, I politely explained to her that my mom had an unusually hard time hearing since she came in to the hospital. Maya then answered with, "I know, I've been her nurse all day."

So I thought to myself, *If you knew, why were you asking her questions she didn't understand/hear?* But that's not what I said to Maya. Instead, I lost my temper and said rather sharply, "Then what was that all about? You knew she couldn't hear most of the words?"

And believe it or not, she responded, "The process says I have to ask her them. I knew most of her answers anyway. It hasn't changed all day."

Are you kidding me? is what I was thinking by that time. Of course it hadn't changed. My mom didn't know what Maya was saying! She smiled and nodded her head with every question she couldn't hear.

And don't get me started on "The process says..." One of my main jobs at work is to help set up process infrastructure for different departments. I deal with processes all the time and all different topics. One of the things that burns me to no end is someone using a process as an excuse for poor behavior. I think my face turns bright red anytime I hear "I did it because the process says so."

At that point in the Maya conversation, I recognized

I was fuming and about to say something not too pleasant. I still tried hard to think positively, and all I came up with was the following positive thought: *She was primarily just asking Mom about her bathroom habits and eating habits. In the grand scheme of things, she was not hurting Mom.*

I was so angry I decided not to vocalize any of my thoughts to Maya. I just shook my head and walked away. In the span of a few short minutes, Maya was able to alter my mood completely and drag my spirits down. I needed to remove myself from the situation before I lost it. She wasn't necessarily being outwardly negative, but her actions created a negative environment for me. I certainly had less energy after that interaction than before I had met her. It clearly illustrated that even a stranger can have a lot of power over your moments.

Just when I thought I had hit my bottom with negativity, I went back to my mom's room. And you can probably guess what Mom said to me: "I told you so. She isn't very nice."

Wasn't that just great? I was frustrated on many levels and then I got an "I told you so." It sure didn't add any positive energy to the moment. Yet I had an interesting reaction. For a brief second I almost joined my mom and gave her ammunition about Maya. At face value, Mom was right. Maya did seem unfriendly, and was not someone I would want caring for me. I had let this stranger suck the energy from me by her laissez-faire attitude, and I was unable to find a speck of positivity in her.

That was when my stubbornness started to rear its ugly head. I was determined not to leave the hospital feeling negative and with less energy than when I had arrived. I also felt that if I left on this note, I would be worried about Mom all night. In addition, I kept thinking of the phrase "nip it in the butt." So after a few minutes of chitchat with Mom, I decided to go and ask Maya a medical question. I found her with her nose in the computer and asked her when Mom's next dose of pain medications was scheduled to be administered.

Maya quickly gave me the answer without ever looking up. I could have turned and left, but I decided to try and "flip the tables." If I was going to "nip this in the butt," it was my last chance. I proceeded with "Maya, I know it must be hard up here with all these patients. I just want you to know that I appreciate you taking care of my mom. My whole family is terribly worried about her."

That expression of gratitude made her raise her eyes from the screen. She said, "Thank you. It is hard. So many sick people here, and I wish I could make all their pain go away, but I can't."

Without even trying, I started to understand her behavior. Maybe she didn't connect too much to her patients because she was afraid if she did, she could get hurt if something happened to them. By strictly following process, she didn't have to bring any emotions or feelings into each interaction with the patients.

Surprisingly, the flood gates opened, and Maya became a chatter box. I found out that she had come to the United States as a child, and her parents didn't speak any English. She put herself through school and worked multiple jobs. She probably didn't have a lot of time to develop a social network and, therefore, probably did not have a lot of time to get close to people. She also had a serious case of pneumonia a few months earlier, and she shared how awful it was. She hated the feeling of not being able to breathe.

As we ended our "get to know you" conversation, Maya assured me she would keep a close eye on my mom throughout the night. Even though Mom couldn't hear her very well, she said she could tell from my mom's expressions how she was doing. So here was this nurse who had only spent eight hours with my mom, and she had already gotten to know her body language. She cared enough to do that to make sure her patients were receiving good care.

Wow, what a turn of events. Sometimes when you try to understand what's causing the perceived negativity, it helps you gain a new perspective on the situation. That wasn't my intent when I went back to find Maya. My real intent was to connect with her a little, so I might feel a bit better when I left the hospital, knowing this woman was looking after my mom.

I would never make excuses for negative behavior. I don't think anyone should be disrespectful to another person, but sometimes when you understand what's actually going on, it takes the "sting" out of the negative situation.

At seemingly negative moments like this, try hard to find one positive thought. That positive thought can help you get to the next one and so on. And before you know it, you'll have "flipped the tables" and turned a negative situation around. You will feel lighter!

The final story in this chapter is about a chance encounter with a phlebotomist who had an uplifting view on life. Her daily motto forced her to look at negative moments from a fresh perspective every time she encountered one. Can you imagine what the world we live in would be like if we all did that? The following story clearly shows that this phlebotomist is the blade of grass that moves with the wind.

How Patient Can You Be?

By Kris

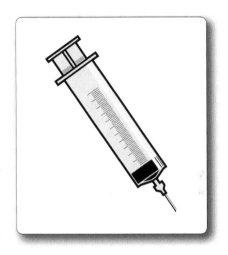

On a particular Friday morning in early May, I had a routine blood work appointment scheduled. It was one that I had booked online, where you have to "click" to accept the terms written in a paragraph, similar to the following:

"I agree to arrive on time. Failure to arrive within five minutes of the appointment will forfeit your appointment. This lab prides itself on running on time and cannot tolerate late arrivals."

I had been to this lab multiple times, and for the most part, it did run on time. So boy was I surprised when I walked in to find standing room only in the waiting room. There were at least twenty-five people waiting. My first thought was that *maybe most of these people are walk-ins, and because I have an appointment, I will be taken first.* I was very proud of my positive in-the-moment thought, until I read the extremely large sign next to the sign-in book:

WE NO LONGER TAKE WALK-IN APPOINTMENTS. YOU MUST HAVE A SCHEDULED APPOINT-MENT FOR THIS FACILITY AS OF 5/1/2012.

I checked the date on my phone. It was May 4, 2012. Hmmm…my positive "in the moment" thought was not so accurate.

Staying positive in moments like these take work for me. I like to take a deep breath (my pause) and analyze my options before I determine a course of action or thought. So at this point, I figured, I had a few different options. I could:

❀ Leave and make a new appointment. That would be a pain. I had to arrange for a sitter for the current appointment and would have to get a sitter again. This option would most likely cause me to feel frustrated.

❀ Be upset and grumble to myself about it for the next hour. All this would do is probably make me feel worse, and it wouldn't make them call my name any faster.

❀ Accept the fact that there must be a reason they are running late and sit down, relax, and watch the *Today* show on television.

Since I had two little ones at home and the bulk of my TV watching consisted of Dora, Barney, and Scooby Doo, I decided the *Today* show wasn't such a terrible choice. I could take this time as a chance to relax and watch some television.

As people walked in, it was funny to watch the expressions on their faces and see how they would handle the situation. It's not often in life where you get to experience a moment, decide how you will react, accept it, and then watch others experience practically the same moment. It took about a minute for a new person to look around the waiting room and realize they had about an hour to wait. I was truly amazed at the reactions. They were all very different, but I noticed one consistent trend — the people who accepted the moment (or the hour) they were facing were clearly more peaceful than those who didn't when they sat down in the waiting room.

The first person to experience the moment was a sweet, older woman with a walker. When she signed in she said to the receptionist, "I see you have quite a crowd. That's okay. At my age, I've learned that this is nothing to fret about. There are much bigger things to worry about these days."

The second person to come in was a retired gentleman who couldn't find his name on the list. It turned out he wasn't on the list because he was two hours early for his appointment! He didn't get upset or frustrated with himself. He laughed it off and said, "My wife always says I have awful handwriting. Guess I didn't write the time down clearly when I booked the appointment. That's okay. I'm going to go watch my grandson get on the bus, have coffee with my daughter, and I'll see you in two hours. Hopefully, you'll be back on schedule by then."

The next man to walk in was undoubtedly my comic relief for the remainder of my wait. He was about seventy-five, and when he walked in, he said loud enough for everyone to hear, "Holy smokes! This is a lot of people!" He signed in and made multiple comments to the receptionist about how they must be behind. She assured him they were doing everything they could to move things along quickly.

The next person to walk through the door was a younger man, who sat down next to my comic relief. It turned out he was the older gentleman's son, who had driven him to the appointment.

As soon as the son sat down, the father loudly asked "Can you believe it? There sure are a lot of people in here."

"It's okay, Dad. We don't have any place to be. I'm sure it won't be too long of a wait. Don't worry about it. Don't let this get your blood pressure going."

"Blood pressure? How can this situation not affect my blood pressure? They're running way behind. Probably means the people don't know what they're doing. I bet this is going to hurt. I'll probably get someone right out of school."

"Dad, please keep your voice down. I'm sure they're just extra busy, and they all know what they're doing. Do you want me to get you a magazine?"

"No, thank you. You might lose your seat if you get up."

"I'm sure I won't lose my seat, Dad. It's okay. I can get you a magazine."

"No, thank you. Too many germs on those things anyway."

As you see, there was a pattern here: This gentleman responded negatively to any moment he was facing. I'm not sure if the wait put him in that frame of mind or if this was his standard MO. Either way, I don't think his reaction was making him feel any better. He would be quiet for a second, until the next person was called into the waiting room.

"Arlene, please." Two women stood up and asked the nurse, "Which Arlene?" "The 7:45 Arlene" the nurse replied.

Well, that just set off the older gentleman behind me. Now he knew exactly how far behind they were and exclaimed, "7:45, It's 8:41! They are 56 minutes behind schedule. How do you get 56 minutes behind?"

"Dad, please be quiet. Everyone can hear you. It's okay. They'll get to us when they get to us."

"I'm not saying anything but the truth. They are 56 minutes behind." Then, in a lowered voice that only us closest to him could hear, he said to his son, "I bet I know what it is now — It's Friday! I've heard about those TGIFs. I bet they are drinking mimosas and celebrating in the back. Do you think she will be drunk when she takes my blood?"

"Dad! No, they are not drinking. They are just behind schedule. It's okay. Watch the TV."

On this last interchange, I couldn't help but start to giggle. This guy was just cracking me up. He was so caught up in the moment and badly needed to understand what was causing the delay. He was stressing himself, his son, others around him too. I, on the other hand, could only see the humor in it and was actually having a good time in the waiting room now. I knew that the situation was making for a good story!

As I continued to giggle, the girl next to me and I made eye contact. She said, "Oh…he is the best one yet."

I whispered how I was actually thinking I was glad they were running late so I could hear the stand-up act behind us. She laughed and continued to tell me she had been there three hours.

"Three hours!" I exclaimed, thinking I had estimated the delay exceedingly poorly. She quickly assured me it wasn't a three-hour wait. She had to take a sugar test and needed to wait three hours before they took some blood from her. I asked her how she had passed the time. She said it was by using her iPad, watching TV, and people watching. She, too, was intrigued by people's reactions.

She told me about some people who came in prior to me. Two of them actually yelled at the receptionist and stormed out. I wondered to myself how they must feel now. Maybe in the heat of the moment it felt good to vent their frustration at someone, but after that moment had passed, I would assume there would be a letdown once they realized they needed to make a new appointment. In the long run, would they truly save an hour? Was it worth it to yell at someone who certainly had no control over the situation?

I eventually was called for my appointment by a sweet woman who immediately apologized for the wait. I asked her what the holdup was, and she relayed to me that the "powers that be" changed the online sign-up to take more appointments within each ten minute window. They put in a new room for blood draws, but never hired a new person to take blood. The woman told me she thought before they hired someone, they wanted to see "how bad" it would get with wait times. She believed the management wanted to see what the patients would tolerate. Since they implemented the new online appointment system, the average wait time was forty-five minutes.

I asked her, "Well, are the patients tolerating it?"

She replied, "I don't think so. Yesterday I actually had to call the police because one man was cursing and yelling so much we were afraid he would get violent."

That just shocked me. I understand being frustrated, but causing a scene over an hour wait? I cannot imagine that type of reaction would make a person feel better once the moment had passed. It seemed that type of behavior would lead to more anger, rather than a feeling of peace.

This was a situation that wasn't even caused by the workers, but they were taking the brunt of all the angry customers. The "powers that be" were sitting in a corporate office somewhere else and making decisions just from numbers.

Thinking about these poor workers who were dealing with grumpy people reminded me again to always take a deep breath, try to step out of the moment, and look at the situation from a different angle. In the grand scheme of things, what's the big deal about waiting an hour? In this case, I didn't have anywhere to go, and the kids were in good hands.

The phlebotomist continued to tell me how much she used to love her job, but she felt the company was now forcing her to hate it. She said she was trying so hard to remain positive, but didn't think she had the strength to do it for much longer. She was so tired of the negative energy of her patients after they waited so long for their appointments.

I asked her what her next step was. She said she thought she had two options, if the situation didn't change:

❀ Stay at the lab and be unhappy, which would probably result in being grouchy to her patients, and that was something she never wanted to do

❀ Find a new job.

At the moment, in a less than ideal situation, she was staying positive for her patients. But she realized that, in the long run, she had to do what was best for her. I told her how strong I thought she was. "Honey, it isn't being strong," she responded. "I probably have twenty more years of living than you do, and in those twenty years, I have come to learn that nothing good comes out of being negative."

When I walked out of that building that morning, I reflected on what a powerful one hour of moments I had just been through. And for each of those moments, her statement rang true to me: "Nothing good comes out of being negative."

❀ ❀ ❀ ❀ ❀ ❀

This book was so fun to write because all of these ideas are fairly straightforward to implement and easily illustrated with examples from real people, who had to work to be positive in each moment. As you've likely come to realize, a slight change of your perception in a moment can seriously alter what you feel emotionally and physically.

You have the power to change a moment just by the way you view it. The blade of grass that moves with the wind is the person who pauses and views the situation from different angles. The blade of grass that goes against the wind is the person who reacts based on their initial view of the moment. That is the person who can't "get out of the forest fire" or can't "see the forest through the trees."

By looking at each moment from a fresh perspective, you can surely "flip the tables" and "nip negativity in the butt." So the key question here is: In your moments, are you nipping negativity in the butt, or is it nipping you?

Chapter 5

Don't Sweat It

Does It Really Matter?

The last chapter focused on looking at negative moments from a different angle to help give you a fresh perspective on a situation. What if you are in a negative moment and you cannot see another angle from which to view it? It's not always so easy to find another perspective. Maybe you just dropped your mail in a mud puddle. What if you burned dinner and the kids are having meltdowns because they're hungry? Have you ever dumped a bag of dog food on the floor? In those instances, it can be hard to find a different angle on the situation. Seriously, what other angle is there other than a big mess if you've just dumped dog food on the floor?

A fresh perspective can give you more energy to stay positive and not get pulled into a negative moment. But just how do you get one of those 'spectives when you're staring at something that feels like it could make you snap or cry? Our suggestion is simply to ask yourself: Does "it" really matter? As in the previous chapters, the "it" here is whatever is causing the negative moment. Whatever the "it" is, will it have a large impact on your life and do you want to waste energy on it in this moment?

❀ Does it really matter that yogurt just got dumped all over the floor? In the grand scheme of things, most likely not. Cleaning it up takes less than five minutes.

❀ Does it really matter that a person just cut in front of you at the grocery store? Probably not. Maybe they have to get home to pick up their child and didn't even see you making your way to the same checkout lane.

❀ Does it really matter that your husband didn't vacuum or wash the floor before the party? Probably not. It is likely no one will notice. They will just be happy to spend time with you and your family.

❀ Does it really matter that the person in front of you at the yellow light chose not to make the left turn, so it caused you to have to stop, too? Probably not. Maybe you could use that extra minute to take a few deep breaths and relax to some music.

When you are feeling your negative vibe indicators creeping up on you, and you cannot think of another perspective for the situation, ask yourself, Does it really matter? How will this situation really impact your life? Will you remember this event in a week, a month, a year? Will the moment have a lasting impact on you? If not, try to take a deep breath, address the situation, and move on. Bringing this thought process into your everyday life can make you happier in the long run. In the following stories, we provide examples of how asking Does it really matter? can soften even the most negative of moments.

The Purple Lock

By Kris

I was in the locker room at the YMCA. A woman I didn't recognize was walking around the room looking at each locker and said to me, "I should have remembered my locker number. Now I'm roaming around trying to find my stuff." I smiled and joked with her that it was good exercise. I also suggested that she could consider buying a unique color lock like mine, which was purple. I shared with her that a purple lock is easy to spot and find at times like these.

At that moment, another woman joined our conversation and said, "You know, I had a purple lock stolen from me here in this locker room once. I set it down for a second and then it was gone. That was the second item stolen from me at this facility. The other item I had taken from me was a Mickey Mouse towel."

My first reaction had me feeling sorry for her. The thought of someone stealing from another also caused me to feel a bit of anger. Stealing goes against all of my core beliefs, which are focused on honesty and respecting others' things. I can almost understand how a person could choose to steal food or money if they were truly desperate. But I have a hard time grasping when someone would steal a non-necessity item like a Mickey Mouse towel or a purple lock. My next thought was *What is this world coming to?* I could feel some negativity brewing up in me and I was preparing myself to have a conversation with this stranger about how horrible some people are. Boy did she surprise me!

I told her, "I'm sorry that happened to you because it must have been very disappointing." And I'll never forget her response.

"I prefer to think that the person desperately needed a purple lock and Mickey Mouse towel for some reason," she replied. "I cannot think of what that reason might be, but that's okay. Sure, I could get caught up in a pity party for myself but to what end? A positive outlook helps me through my moments of anger and brings me peace. And in the grand scheme of things, did it really matter that I lost a towel and a lock? Nope."

I was so pleasantly surprised by this stranger's response, and I could immediately feel our conversation shift, and that it was going to be upbeat rather than negative. I told her it was refreshing to hear such a positive attitude. We continued to chat for about five minutes about how it feels when you are positive versus negative. We discussed how hard it can be to stay positive when a lot of the world seems quite the opposite. However, when you stay positive, you usually feel better after the moment is over. As our conversation continued, you could tell we were both getting more energized with every comment. It is truly an uplifting feeling to have a conversation with someone where you talk about seeing the positive in every moment. We introduced ourselves at the end of the conversation, and I truly hope my path will cross with Stephanie's again. I know that she's making an impression on everyone she meets, and I hope that this lesson will help me do the same.

❀ ❀ ❀ ❀ ❀ ❀

Stephanie's story shows how someone who could have felt sorry for herself or negative about the whole situation managed to stay upbeat about it. She asked herself if it really mattered, and when she assessed it, losing her towel and lock did not impact her life in any major way. She made a decision to stay positive and not let the poor decisions of someone else bring her down. When she told the story, she was able to fill me with hope and positivity. That sure feels better than being pulled down by someone's negative outlook.

In the next story, Jeanie smells a negative moment coming on, and she asks herself if it really matters. With her answer to the question, she truly nips the potential negative moment in the butt!

To Tip or Not to Tip?

By Jeanie

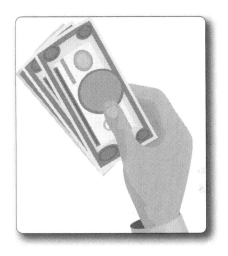

It goes without saying that people in your life will want to help you out at certain times by offering you advice sometimes. Not that you necessarily want such advice, but they'll share it with you anyway.

Most of the time, I can handle it well, and I will try and listen to what they say and many times I will incorporate my family or friends' advice into my decision-making process. Sometimes though, people may use a tone or a word that sets off my negative indicators. I never realized one of my hot buttons until Kris once pointed out to me the danger of using the word "should" when talking to others. For example:

❀ "You should get your hair cut."

❀ "You should go to Florida."

❀ "You should try that restaurant."

❀ "You should discipline your child with a time out."

❀ "You should take that promotion."

❀　"You should lease the car, not buy it."

❀　"You should paint your wall red."

One of the definitions of "should" is that it is used to indicate obligation, duty, or correctness, typically when criticizing someone's actions. So you can see how if I were to say, "You should brush your hair" it would sound like I am criticizing either your hair or the way you look. It feels as if someone is telling you what to do. When I hear the word used in that context now, the hair on my neck stands a little taller.

Since Kris brought this to my attention, I have tried to be more cognizant of my use of the word and am much more sensitive to it when others use it. This is a straightforward story of when an acquaintance of mine used the "should" word. If I had not been aware of the "should" word, our conversation may have taken an entirely different path.

A year or so ago, I was on a bicycling trip and had quickly made some new friends. We had a terrific time each and every day. The trip was a thoroughly positive experience, each of us enjoying the riding, the sightseeing, and supporting one another as we attained new personal goals. On the last day, we stopped for a quick lunch. The waitress had provided good service, and we each had separate checks. In my mind, the bill was small, less than twenty dollars, so I gave the waitress a five dollar tip. I have no idea what the others gave the waitress. I genuinely don't care about those things because I feel that it's none of my business. Obviously, one of the other riders cared because this is how the conversation went:

"How much was your dinner?" she asked.

"I don't know," I replied. "About $20."

"Why did you tip so much?" she then inquired.

"I believe in trickle-down economics," I said, laughing, but of course I was just joking. I like to be generous in my life, yet I don't like a lot of attention about it.

"No, really, why did you tip her so much?" she continued to press.

"I'm comfortable financially, and I can't take it with me," was my honest response. "I don't have kids to leave it to, and I like helping others who may not be as fortunate as I am."

By her body language and facial expressions, I knew she wasn't comfortable with my words. For some reason, my higher than average tip set off something in her. She started to lecture me about how 10-15% was standard. She went on to explain that maybe with outstanding service she could see 20%, but 25% seemed a bit extreme. Her next two statements are what caused "an uneasy feeling" in my stomach and put my negative senses in alert mode.

"You should tip the average amount," she added. "You shouldn't tip so much."

Immediately, I felt the hair on my neck stand up. I wanted to snap back and say, "Why shouldn't I tip that much?" But had I said that, we would have wound up in some type of negative debate that just wouldn't end well. Instead, I took a deep breath, paused, and thought to myself, *Does this really matter?* The answer in my mind was *No, it doesn't matter that she cannot understand why you would tip 25%. Don't engage with her. Let it go. Maybe she is just tired and cranky from the day's ride and doesn't even realize she sounds like she is picking a fight.*

So rather than give her something to work with, I just sat silently as we rode back to the hotel. She kept trying to engage me by her attempts to make more points on the subject, but I just listened quietly. After she went on for a few minutes, I changed the subject. Our conversation moved on to what a fantastic trip we had and where we would go next year. It was much nicer to end our trip and our last lunch on a positive conversation about something to look forward to rather than an unnecessary debate about how much money to tip.

❀ ❀ ❀ ❀ ❀ ❀

Anytime you are feeling you may be pulled into a negative situation, it helps to access the impact this has on your life. In this case, Jeanie realized her fellow cyclist was probably just having an "off moment." It wasn't worth it to Jeanie to engage in a negative debate. Instead, Jeanie realized this moment would not impact her life in any way. She took the high road, put an end to the conversation, and moved forward. Sometimes that's what friends do for each other!

In the next story, Kris relates her experience on a particularly rainy day, and how her two-year-old daughter showed her that sometimes it just doesn't matter if you're soaking wet. It's still important to take time to stop and catch raindrops on your tongue!

A Rainy Day

By Kris

Here I was on a Tuesday afternoon. I had left work later than normal due to a meeting running late. The weather forecaster had been predicting rain all day, but Mother Nature decided to hold off just until I was about to walk out of the building. I did not have my umbrella with me, so I was happy that it was just drizzling. Yet I hadn't taken ten steps and it started to rain harder... and harder. Within seconds it hit the "sideways rain" stage, when the wind kicks up and the rain feels as if it is coming sideways. There is no escaping sideways rain, not even with an umbrella.

By the time I got in the car, I looked like I had decided to take a swim in my work clothes. I tried hard to push the negative thoughts out of my head and appreciate the rain. After all, it was watering my plants and replenishing our Great Lakes.

My first stop was five minutes away, to pick up my daughter at day care. I ran the heater on the highest speed to try and dry myself out, but it was not particularly successful.

When I got to day care, I stepped out of the car and into a three-inch-deep puddle. You may be asking "Didn't you look down?" Well of course I did, but the rain was still coming at me sideways. It was pelting my face and my eyes at a disturbing rate, and it was hard to see where the ground was. Hence, I stepped into a deep puddle! So now my shoes, socks, and bottom of my pants were soaked. It was the kind of soaked that requires you to wring out your socks and pants in order to even start the drying process!

My positive attitude was taking a nose dive pretty quickly, but I was still holding on (even if it was by a thread) by taking a few deep breaths. I was hoping to walk down the hall, pick up my daughter, and get out unnoticed. Yeah, right! Who was I kidding?

I looked miserable enough with being wet, but the noise coming from me was unlike any I had ever heard. There was a swishy-swashy squeak coming out of my shoes and socks that could be heard throughout the building. Of course, my daughter's room was the last one down the hall. I had to pass seven rooms and fourteen teachers, most of whom I know on a first-name basis. You can imagine the comments I heard as I walked down the hall.

"Is it raining that hard out there?"

"Did you lose your umbrella?"

"Wow! You must have been caught in the storm at the wrong time."

"Gotta a little wet, did you?"

"Kris, what happened to you?"

With every step I felt my mood spiraling in the wrong direction. I seriously expected to hit bottom with my attitude, and I planned to have a grumpy rest of the night. Even though that sounded like a bad option, there was no amount of breathing or pausing that could turn my thought process around at that moment.

I did not see any other angle to this situation, and when I asked myself, *Does this really matter?* the answer came from my negative side. *Yes, it matters. You are sopping wet and the talk of the day care. People will remember this for a long time.* Looking back at the situation, it really wasn't a big deal, but in the moment my attitude was negative and there was no flipping my tables, or at least so I thought.

I finally reached my daughter and she gave me her traditional "running/leaping into my arms hug" yelling, "My mommy is here!" In hindsight, you would think I would have snapped out of my mood immediately. But I just couldn't quite get there because, remember, with every step I took, my shoes squeaked and reminded me of my predicament. As we walked out of the building, any teacher who missed my walk of wetness on the way in got a chance to see me now on the way out. Word spreads quickly in a small day care facility. They just had to check out what happened to Kris. I tried hard to smile and laugh with them, but for the most part, all I could do was shake my head.

My daughter and I finally got outside, and it was still raining. I immediately snapped at her and said, "Come on, we have to hurry, so you don't get wet." But she slowed down even more, just like a two-year-old does when a parent encourages them to speed up. Toddlers have no concept of "hurrying." My thoughts were not pleasant at that moment, and I felt another sharp voice coming. But when I looked down at her, she was looking up at me with her tongue sticking out of her mouth.

"Mommy, if we go fast, we can't catch the raindrops on our tongues! Who cares if I get wet? This is more fun!"

Instantly, every negative thought melted away. I stood with her and we caught raindrops on our tongues. She got wet and so what? We both eventually dried out, and we shared a moment that I will never forget. That's truly what matters.

❀ ❀ ❀ ❀ ❀ ❀

Sometimes, when you get caught up in a negative spiral, it truly does help when someone else can pull you out of the moment. In this case, it took a two-year-old's perspective to change a forty-year-old's mood. Children truly can teach you to live in the moment and can show that some things just don't matter.

Since we just finished one "wet" story, let's look at another incident where Kris' six-year-old son shows us how to use the "it just doesn't matter" technique in everyday situations. He also demonstrates that laughter almost always brings a new perspective.

As Simple as Dry Underwear

By Kris

Jeanie and I live in two different states, so as we wrote this book, we had weekly meetings to discuss the book and assign what we called "our home-work" for the week. Most weeks we met on Sunday nights, right after bedtime for my kids. With this schedule, we had a better chance to have some quiet time while we worked. Before each meeting, I would get my office all set up with a fancy glass full of water, a small bowl of snacks, candles, and relaxing music. This helped me decompress from the normal craziness and got me focused to work on the book. On most nights, my son Matthew would still be awake while I was getting ready to meet with Jeanie.

During the first few weeks of this routine, he wanted to know what I was doing. A simple answer of "I'm work-ing with Miss Jeanie tonight" would satisfy his curiosity. But as the weeks went on, each Sunday he wanted to know a little bit more.

One week it was "What are you and Miss Jeanie working on?" I told him, "Miss Jeanie and I are writing a book."

When I tell an adult that Jeanie and I are writing a book, they are genuinely surprised and want more details.

I don't think it's particularly common for most people to write a book, and the concept intrigues most folks. For a six year old, there is nothing funny or strange about it. He reads books all the time with Mommy, so why wouldn't she write a book? It's probably just as normal to him as Mommy making dinner.

He thought about the whole book writing thing and the following week he wanted to know more about it. This is how our conversation went:

"Mommy, what kind of book are you writing?"

"A book that tells people how Mommy tries to stay happy all the time."

"Not a book about trucks? Trucks make me happy."

"I know you love trucks, but this book is to help adults not get mad so easily."

"Mommy, you aren't happy when I don't listen. Will you tell people I don't listen?"

"No, Matthew. I won't tell them that, but I will tell them about all the things you do that make me smile and laugh. How is that?"

"Okay, Mommy, but when you are done with that, will you write me a truck book?"

The next week during my set up routine, he asked, "Mommy, why are you writing the book?" As you can see, the questions were getting harder each week. It seemed his little wheels were spinning in his head, and he was genuinely trying to figure this all out.

It was challenging trying to think of ways to explain to a six-year-old what Jeanie and I were doing. How do you convey staying positive in the moment to a child, when all they do is live positively in the moment? Children immediately forget about everyday negative moments and move on to the next moment, as if nothing negative ever happened. A child is the true epitome of living in the moment.

I answered his question with the following:

"I want to make people laugh and show them how I try to stay happy. Maybe that will help someone who is sad."

"Mommy," he responded. "Does the book help you when you are sad about Grandma?"

My mom had recently passed away and Matthew was still trying to understand the whole concept of losing someone.

"Writing the book does help me, and do you know why? I may be sad sometimes because I miss her, but most of the time I am happy because I have so many memories of Grandma in my heart. When I write the book, I remember to try and stay happy and not sad."

"Okay Mommy. Maybe I can think of something happy to make people smile."

A month or so went by, and I didn't get anymore questions from Matthew during the set up routine. I thought he had forgotten about the book. That was not the case. When he came home from school one day, he ran inside and changed into a bathing suit while I set up the sprinkler. He, Sara, and I played outside and shared a lot of laughs. It was a beautiful day, and there is nothing like hearing the laughs of children running through the sprinkler. I truly savored the moment and thought about nothing else during that time. It was the kids' first time using the sprinkler for the summer, and they were thoroughly enjoying themselves.

After an hour or so, we went inside so I could start dinner. I asked Matthew to change in the bathroom and to come to the kitchen when he was done. As I started dinner, I heard him giggling a little, and he bounced into the kitchen with a laugh that only a kindergartener can express. Immediately, I knew something was up.

"Mommy, look!" he said with a very silly grin on his face.

I took a look, and nothing seemed out of place. All he had on was underwear. That would be the first step in getting dressed, so I did not catch on to what he was trying to show me.

"Mommy, look closer."

That's when I realized his underwear was wet— completely sopped, as if he had been swimming (or running through a sprinkler for an hour). I laughed out loud when I realized what had happened.

"Mommy, I guess I was so excited to go in the sprinkler, I forgot to take my underwear off. That is funny, right mommy? Would that make people laugh? Maybe you can write a story about that? It is making you laugh."

"I sure can, Buddy, and you know what else? It's okay that your underwear is wet. You had so much fun outside."

His next response showed that in his own young way he understood that certain things don't need to make you upset or negative. Certain things just don't matter in the grand scheme of things.

"Mommy, accidents happen sometimes, right? And when they do, we don't yell. All I have to do is get a dry pair of underwear from upstairs, right?"

Sometimes, through the eyes of a child, life appears so uncomplicated. Also, I'm amazed at how young children truly understand positivity. That is their one angle on situations. He wasn't worried that I would yell. He knew deep down, from the values he has seen in our house, that it was no big deal, and we could smile about it. It was a powerful moment! It just didn't matter that his underwear was wet.

❀ ❀ ❀ ❀ ❀ ❀

Take a moment to reflect on how you would have reacted if that situation happened in your home. Would you have been angry that his underwear was wet and thought he should have been more careful? Would you have laughed right along with him and understood that it really didn't matter because there was such an easy fix? In the grand scheme of your life, is a situation like this really worth getting irritated or upset over?

Your response to a situation can ultimately define the mood of everyone in it. Kris sure liked the mood of her family during dinner that night and would not have wanted it to be any other way!

In the next story, Jeanie provides an example of recognizing the negativity of a situation and choosing her reaction to it (with a little help from a four-legged friend), in turn, making it positive.

The Futon Mattress

By Jeanie

I have had a lot of dogs over the years, and each one becomes part of my family. As with people, every dog has a distinct personality. I currently have three dogs. The old man of the crew is Ditto. He is a Beagle/Terrier mix. He loves playing ball and Frisbee. And although he is afraid of new things and new people, he is a loving and gentle dog.

The middle one is Webster. He is a large, fluffy Golden Retriever/black Lab mix. While he is not the smartest dog, he exceptionally loves anyone who comes into his world. His smile and eyes will melt anyone's heart, even someone who doesn't like dogs.

And finally, the "baby" of the group is Sidney, an English Setter. He is a loner, preferring to patrol the yard in case we are attacked by a blood-thirsty flock of birds or a vicious bunny rabbit.

These dogs bring so much joy to my life, but as you can imagine with three medium-to-large dogs, they also can bring chaos. On this particular day, I decided I was going to clean out my car. In the back of the car I have a futon mattress for the dogs to lie on when we take long car trips. The mattress cover was dirty from a recent trip to visit my folks, so I removed the cover and washed it.

The mattress was about five feet by six feet in size. I didn't want the dogs lying on the unprotected mattress in the house, so I put it on the deck outside where there was more room. Also, when the dogs go outside, they are so interested in what animals they can chase or what new smells they can investigate, I figured they wouldn't even notice the mattress on the deck. That theory flew out the window when I looked out and saw Sidney having the time of his life ripping the mattress to pieces. The mattress was more fun than any rabbit or squirrel, and as a bonus for Sidney, the mattress didn't run away like animals do!

After a few attempts of me calling Sidney off the mattress, he reluctantly gave up and came in the house for his scolding. My blood was starting to boil, but I kept myself composed and went out to see if I could salvage the mattress. I was thinking that maybe I could still fit the pieces of the mattress into the cover, and it would be suitable for the dogs.

Well, that theory did not pan out, either. Guess who else found out that ripping mattresses was fun? Good old Webster! I am sure he was thinking *If Sidney had a chance, why not me?*

My initial reaction was frustration and anger. But then I looked at Ditto, the wise old man of the group sitting off to the side. He was just watching and taking it all in. No emotion was showing on his face at all. I'm sure he was wondering how much trouble Webster was going to be in. I could almost hear his mind working: *This is great. More treats for me tonight!* Watching Ditto's calm attitude reminded me to remain calm, stop, take a breath, and think. And I did just that.

I knew it was at this point I had to make a choice. Stew about it, yell at the dogs, ruin my day, or make a conscious choice to look at this positively. My first thought was to yell at the dogs, but they don't know any better. While looking at the mess they made, I decided to laugh about it instead. I went inside, did a little research, and ordered a better mattress online. I ordered a lighter and easier to handle mattress that actually worked out better for us, and all the dogs got treats that night!

I realized that out of everything in my life, both good and bad, this just wasn't that awful. The dogs got a new bed, so they are happy. I got a mattress that I can more easily move from the basement to the car when I need it, so I'm happy. Sometimes you have to stop and ask yourself, *Does this really matter?* and decide how you're going to let a situation affect you.

❀ ❀ ❀ ❀ ❀ ❀

It truly is incredible where you can draw calmness from in different situations. The more you look for it, the more you will find it. The help may come from another adult, a child, or in this case, even a dog. The key is to make a decision to seek calmness, and not fuel to add to an already negative situation.

In the next story, Kris comes awfully close to flipping the tables for a stranger by using the Does it really matter? technique. Sometimes though, people choose to remain negative and there is nothing you can do about it.

Grandma at the DMV

By Kris

It was November 2011, and I went to the Department of Motor vehicles (DMV) to obtain my enhanced driver's license. It doesn't mean I'm a better driver, it's the license that allows U.S. citizens to enter Canada without a passport. Over the last several years, there have been a lot of budget cuts in Western New York, and the DMV has shut down many offices. If you thought the perception of long lines was bad before, going to the DMV now has become an all-day adventure.

Based on advice I received from many folks, I planned to arrive fifteen minutes prior to the doors opening. I was a bit surprised when I pulled in the parking lot and it was already half full. I looked around for a twenty-four-hour diner or mini-mart. Nothing was there except the DMV and a Chinese buffet that opened at 10:00 am. It was a brisk morning, and I noticed there was a person in every car. I assumed each person was waiting for the doors to open. I quickly counted and there were fifty cars. That means fifty people would be getting in line soon. I parked and wondered if I should get out of my car. No one else was getting out. Is there DMV etiquette? No one briefed me about this.

I waited a respectable two minutes to open my door.

There were still ten minutes before the DMV opened its doors. As I stepped out of my car, I realized all eyes were on me. All drivers shut off their engines. All doors opened. It was as if I started a domino effect. I picked up my pace a bit because now there were bodies everywhere. I had never seen anything like this before. It was a race to the door! I got to the door with only three people ahead of me and almost fifty behind me. I was pretty proud of myself. I would have been third in line, but the sweetest older woman was next to me and I gave her the space to take the third position. She looked a bit like Betty White— all smiles, sweet, and innocent. She appeared to be the type of woman you would be proud to call your grandmother.

Grandma and I chatted in line a little about the weather and the amount of people in line. She told me it was busy because it was the end of the month.

"Everyone is trying to complete their paperwork before it expires."

Okay, I thought. *I don't know if it's true or not, but I'll go with it.* She sounded like she was a frequent customer. I was thinking she was someone I should stick close to. After all, I was going to need help navigating inside. Through the glass windows, I saw at least one hundred chairs and electronic signs with arrows and numbers in every corner of the room. It looked like something you would see in a train station. The DMV sure had changed in the last decade.

Grandma proceeded to tell me why she was a DMV frequent customer. She had been trying to get her enhanced driver's license as well, and she had attempted to do this on two other occasions, but each time she had been turned away. The first time she had forgotten her proof of residency. On her second visit, she didn't bring her original birth certificate, which it clearly states on all of the paperwork is required. Grandma said she was so old, and her birth certificate was so fragile she didn't want it to leave her house. She believed the clerk should have understood and just accepted the copy she had brought with her. I gently told her they couldn't do that because they are trying to avoid forgery.

"What in heaven would I try to forge?" she asked me. "There is hardly anyone alive as old as me, and I am not a terrorist."

Oh, boy. The conversation was not going as planned. I had just insulted Grandma, and she thought I believed her to be a terrorist! I told her I wasn't implying she was a terrorist, but the DMV employees needed to be fair with the rules and apply them to everyone the same. Grandma let out an expletive at that point. She sure woke up everyone in line with her language.

Now I was extra intrigued and had to ask her what she was doing there for a third visit. She said she caved in and was bringing her fragile birth certificate; and then this whole saga would be over and she would be well on her way to the casino in Niagara Falls, Canada!

When the DMV doors finally opened, everyone in line was split into different groups. I ended up in the same section as Grandma. She was called first. She appeared to be the sweetest person as she explained her predicament to the clerk. Then, I saw her hand her birth certificate over to the clerk who then called the front line supervisor, and I thought *Uh oh. This can't be good for my new friend.*

I heard Grandma's voice rise a bit. "What? Why? I did what you said. Are you kidding me? Do you seriously think I would fake a crumbling, ripped birth certificate to get my license? I am seventy-nine years old, for crying out loud."

The clerk and supervisor wisely decided to call in the

big guns. This sweet woman was quickly spiraling down in the moment. As they walked away to get the manager, who resided in the office area, Grandma turned to me and said, "They say they can't use this because they can't read the date. It's seventy-nine years old! What do they expect?"

I tried to bring out my best attitude "It's okay, it will all work out."

"Easy for you to say," she replied. "I could die tomorrow, especially if this place keeps adding this stress to me."

I was determined to remain positive. "In the big picture, this certainly is not a big deal. It's more of an inconvenience."

At first it seemed Grandma did not like my thought process. She promptly used another expletive. Grandma was clearly not like any grandma I knew!

So, being the eternal optimist, I kept trying to help her see the situation in a more positive light. "Don't you think you'll forget about this in a few months? It's a pain in your 'expletive' now, but you'll deal with it no matter what the manager says. I am sure there will be a way for you to get your license, even if it means another trip back here."

She paused, and I thought I had broken through to her.

"You're right. I will probably laugh about this someday."

"Of course you will," I responded. "Next week you'll be joking about it."

"Don't go crazy," Grandma retorted. "Maybe in a year. But you are right. This is just a small bump, and it isn't worth my energy to get worked up."

We smiled, and I thought she was good. What a course correction at work! I was feeling particularly proud of myself to have helped Grandma in the moment.

However, that elation quickly changed.

The manager came to the window and started her sentence with the dreaded words: "I am sorry, ma'am, but..." It turned out the DMV couldn't take her birth certificate; the date was illegible. As the manager attempted to tell Grandma she could request a new birth certificate, Grandma replied, "You can keep your enhanced driver's license, and you can keep your dumb 'expletive' rules for proof. I guess I just won't go to Canada before I die! You are keeping me a hostage in my own country."

With that, Grandma grabbed her paperwork and purse and stormed off. And she didn't even glance back my way. My Grandma friend was gone. There was no positiveness in that moment.

Although the moment changed for a second with Grandma, the positivity didn't stick to help her through her next negative moment. She must have not truly believed it would be okay, no matter what the outcome. It isn't an easy thing to stay positive in every moment. It takes a lot of energy, and sometimes we just won't have the energy to do it. That's okay.

There's always next time!

❀ ❀ ❀ ❀ ❀ ❀

Reflect for a second about how you feel when you're in a negative moment. Do you feel out of control? Do you feel tired and zapped of energy? Do you feel upset, angry, or sad? Does your stomach or head hurt? Most people would never choose to feel any of these emotions or physical pain. We believe that most people want to feel happy, uplifted, and full of energy. Trying to stay positive as much as possible will help you with all of these things. It does take some work, but in the end it is totally worth it.

The next story illustrates that something very simple can cause negativity. It may seem far-fetched, but we're sure everyone has a story or two like this where a minor, insignificant event starts a negative spiral. Are you able to realize what's going on and nip the negativity in the butt?

The Tabs

By Kris

People who know me probably would categorize me as fairly mild mannered, as I do not get angry much and I hardly ever raise my voice (except maybe with the kids). Yet there are a few things that can push me over the edge. One of them is if I feel pressured with a deadline for work.

Years ago, I had to prepare for an all-day meeting with a large group of senior managers. I had spent many hours preparing material and planning for the day. On the afternoon before the meeting, all I had to do was assemble the binders for each participant. I expected it to be easy and thought it would be a good project with which to wrap up the day. What I didn't expect was that I had to insert pieces of paper with the section names into several tabbed cardboard separators in the binders.

There were about twenty binders with ten separators each. Many of the paper inserts were larger than the holders, so each small piece of paper had to be trimmed. I'm sure you're thinking *Why didn't you just print a new sheet of labels? Well,* the person who had created the sheet had gone home for the day, and I, in my infinite wisdom, thought it would be faster to trim the labels for each tab.

A coworker noticed my dilemma and offered to help. It was apparent my plan was not working. It was literally taking us minutes to insert a paper label into each sep-arator. I was getting more frustrated with every tick of the clock. Most people had gone home by this time, and I just wanted the project to be over. We weren't even a quarter of the way through.

My coworker continued to try and calm me, offer-ing other solutions to no avail. I wasn't listening, and I was determined to do it my way. Remember, I have a strong stubborn streak in me. Was my reaction rational? Absolutely not. But once that negativity comes nipping, sometimes it opens the door and makes itself at home. The result is an irrational woman muttering under her breath about the tabs.

Finally, when my frustration was at its peak, I took a binder, turned it upside down, and started shaking it crazily like a wild woman. And I exclaimed, "I hate these tabs! What was I thinking?" (Note: There may have been a few expletives in the actual sentences.)

My coworker was shocked to see "reserved Kris" lose it and she burst out laughing. As I realized what I must have looked like and saw all my tab inserts crumbled and lying at my feet, I snapped out of it. I conceded and said, "Now what are we going to do?" Her suggestion was to forget the inserts. The actual physical divider was sufficient. These were senior managers. They were smart enough to find the next section in the binder as we pro-gressed through the day.

The meeting did go well, and no one noticed that the sections in the binder were not labeled. This experience provided my coworker and me with many laughs over the years as we reminisced about the day I snapped and dumped tabs all over the floor.

In hindsight, the whole issue of tabs in a binder seems trivial. Kris realized it was ludicrous to get so worked up over some little pieces of paper that would not fit in the holders. In reality, though, this happens to all of us. It's okay. That's a great time to really ask yourself, What impact does this have on my life, not my day or week, but my life? or Will I even remember this a week, month, or year from now? Many times by asking these questions, we can assess the significance of the negative moment and can often see that it's not that important when we view it from a long-term perspective.

Try hard not to stew about the negative moment. Instead, try to laugh about it and move forward. And, recognize that it will happen again. After all, we are human and have a wide range of emotions that are not always easily controlled. Embrace who you are, what you are feeling, and remember to breathe. Moments like these always pass. Very often, when you look back on the situation, you will realize that it was not an earth-shattering event, and will most likely not have an impact on your life.

To wrap up this chapter, Jeanie will share a story that combines the idea of Does it really matter? with those previously discussed concepts of recognizing the negative moment and pausing.

The Parking Situation

By Jeanie

My friend, Jamie, and her sister, Kim, were visiting Kim's son in Georgetown. Jamie lives on the West Coast, so we don't get to see each other that often. Her coming to Georgetown, within thirty-five miles of my house, presented a fantastic opportunity to see her, and I was truly looking forward to the visit.

We made plans to meet at a restaurant in Georgetown. Although I had lived near Baltimore for about six years, I had never been to Georgetown, so I did not know what to expect. Jamie mentioned that they thought there was a parking lot near the restaurant, and she believed the restaurant offered valet parking. My office is roughly sixty miles from the restaurant, and considering DC traffic, I left at about 4:30 p.m. for a 6:30 p.m. dinner. I was hoping two hours would give me plenty of time to arrive on schedule and maximize my short visit with Jamie.

Traffic wasn't too bad, and I was near the restaurant by about 6:15 p.m. I was very pleased, as I do not like driving in heavy traffic at all. On the way there, I decided I would use the restaurant's valet parking. Since I cannot parallel park, I needed to avoid parallel parking on the street, if the regular parking lot was full.

Driving into Georgetown reinforced my decision to

use valet parking, as the traffic was extremely heavy and it was difficult to maneuver. I turned onto the street where the restaurant was located and continued past the parking lot to the restaurant. There was no valet parking option.

I thought to myself, *No problem, I will just go up the street, turn around, and come back.* Well, if you've ever driven in Georgetown on a weeknight at 6:30 p.m., you can attest that the streets are too narrow, and the traffic is too heavy just to drive up the street and turn around.

I could not turn around, so I tried to drive around the block, but I ended up being forced to go farther away from the restaurant on Canal Street, which is a main street. I ended up about two miles away before I could get the car turned around! The traffic was moving at an extremely slow pace. At one point I sat through the same light eight times! And as I've mentioned, I absolutely hate traffic!

It was taking forever to get to the restaurant, so I texted Jamie that I would be late. I was really disappointed because we didn't have a lot of time to visit and catch up, and here I was stuck in traffic. It took me forty-five minutes to get back to the restaurant, and by the time I got there I was mad, upset, and frustrated. You name a negative feeling and I was experiencing it.

I walked in the restaurant and knew I had to shake "it," but how? Then it came to me. As soon as I got to the table, I hugged Jamie and Kim and excused myself to go to the ladies' room. I walked into the ladies' room and took a deep breath. I rolled my shoulders back to release some tension and started looking at this from another angle.

I rarely get to see Jamie. Was I going to let the evening be spoiled by focusing on this negative drive that was in the past? I couldn't undo it. I couldn't change it. It happened and now it was over. The best thing I could do was to let it go so I could thoroughly enjoy my evening with Jamie and Kim. I stood in front of the mirror, looked myself directly in the eyes, and said, "Let it go." I immediately felt the tension leave my body. It was replaced by the excitement of seeing Jamie. I walked out of the ladies' room a different person and the three of us had a fabulous dinner.

❀ ❀ ❀ ❀ ❀ ❀

Stop and ask yourself Does it really matter?" That's one way of trying to find a different angle from which to view the situation. Most moments are actually just a little blip on your entire life's radar. They will eventually be absorbed by other moments and forgotten.

Think about it. Do you remember the last time you spilled something or the last time a friend made you angry? What matters is how happy you are in your life. Do you smile a lot or do you frown? Do you have good friends and family surrounding you? Are you healthy? These are the types of things that truly matter in life. Try not to let the little bumps throw you off course. Always focus on what is truly valuable and important. This will lead you to happier moments every day.

Chapter 6

Accept It

*Finding Peace in a
Negative Moment*

In the last few chapters, we talked about looking at situations from different angles. Some techniques were demonstrated to help you find a fresh perspective, including asking yourself Does it really matter? when you're faced with a not so positive moment. Sometimes, though, certain negative situations really do matter and they are just negative. There is no "flipping the tables" or "nipping negativity in the butt" at those times.

Maybe someone is hurt and needs immediate

medical attention. What if there is a fire at work and everyone needs to be evacuated? There is no stopping the force of Mother Nature, and a weather related event may threaten your family and friends. These are examples of negative moments that you have to deal with and can't be nipped.

All is not lost, though. With practice, you will be able to find a sense of peace in some negative moments, and that will help you deal with them. You won't be able to stop them from being negative, but you'll be able to get through those moments more calmly. As we mentioned in the introduction, we are talking about "smaller" moments. And for this chapter, we're focusing on how to find peace in a short-term moment.

How do you currently react in those truly negative moments that cannot be flipped? Do you lose your composure and become unglued? Or are you someone who remains calm and is able to deal with whatever you are facing? A few years ago, Kris' son fell into a fire pit with hot ashes. He had second degree burns on his hand. Her initial reaction when she saw Matthew was "thank goodness it wasn't his face." Though confronted with a negative situation, she found a moment of peace. That peace didn't fix the moment, but it did help calm her. With that calmness, she was able to stay focused and concentrate on what was best for Matthew during the next few hours.

When a negative situation arises, sometimes you have to dig deep in yourself to find some peace. If you can grab onto just a little bit of it, you'll most likely handle the situation better and be able to help those around you.

In this first story, Jeanie shares how Internet advice helped families find peace during a recent hurricane.

Sanity during Sandy

(and other weather related stories)

By Jeanie

During the fall of 2012, Hurricane Sandy was bearing down on the mid-Atlantic coast. In Maryland they were predicting power outages and downed trees. They were warning everyone to be prepared and to stay safe. I was worried about the possibility of some exceptionally large dead trees in my neighbors' yards falling down on my house. Rather than sleeping upstairs in the bedroom, I decided the safest place to sleep was in my home office on the first floor. If a tree did fall and crash on the house, hopefully it wouldn't make its way to the first floor.

In the office, I set up three dog beds (one for each boy) and a makeshift bed about the size of a twin bed on the floor for me. I left the room for a few minutes to get flashlights and other supplies. When I returned, all three dogs were camped out on my bed, while the dog beds sat empty. I understood that they were frightened by the storm, so I figured out a way for all of us to squeeze together on the makeshift bed. It was not exactly comfortable, but certainly cozy! However, that's not the subject of my story.

I had a generator running, so I was able to connect my computer to the Internet. While we were all nestled in the office, I did some research on the Web regarding the best thing to do when there is a danger of trees falling.

While searching, I came across a post by a mother who was concerned for the safety of her children, and wanted to keep them protected from falling trees. She planned to take them to the basement to sleep, but was afraid of scaring them. Someone replied to her with what I thought was sage advice. This person suggested making a "campout party" in the basement, with sleeping bags, games, snacks, and other fun activities. What a great idea for turning a potentially negative, scary situation into a fun time! While the family was facing a negative event, they could find some moments of peace by having a little adventure. Who knows... maybe the campout in my office brought the dogs a sense of peace during Sandy.

Another storm related incident years ago involved a severe snowstorm in Western New York. (What else is new?) This storm dropped about thirty-six inches of snow over a narrow band of the area in just a few hours. This all happened during the day while most people were still at work. I, along with many of my coworkers, had not paid much attention to the snow accumulation levels. Buffalo snowplowing is amazing and not much halts the area. By the time we realized this was not an average heavy snow-storm, it was too late to get out of the parking lot. Most of the cars were stuck because the parking lot had not been plowed. The roads weren't cleared well because there was so much traffic on them and the plows couldn't do their jobs. Many of us went outside and working together, dug out the cars in the parking lot. But even after six hours, the roads were still impassable. We were stuck there at least for the night. This was definitely a negative situation and we were not going to be able to flip the tables.

We were away from our families during this storm, and not sure when we would be able to travel home. Yet even though we were "stuck", there was a sense of peace because we were safe, protected from the elements, and we had electricity. Amazingly, everyone who was left at work pulled together and started sharing food they had stashed in their desks. Some folks helped others create makeshift beds. People who were stranded in the streets came in, and we found a way to accommodate them so they could be out of the weather. It was a bad situation, but everyone kept a positive attitude (one that I have always found in Western New York) and did everything they could to help one another. We were all able to get home the next day, but it's a night I will always remember.

A final weather related story that I would like to share happened one February when I was still living in Western New York. A bad ice storm had come through the area and knocked out power for thousands of residents, including me. The ice storm was immediately followed by warmer temperatures, so the ice melted quickly. I had a gas fireplace, but it worked with an electric starter, so my only source of heat was a gas oven (and three dogs). To make matters worse, since the electricity was out, my sump pump wasn't working and my basement flooded. You can imagine the frame of mind this situation created for me.

Even though my negative vibe indicators kicked into high gear, I knew I had to dig deep and stay as positive as I could. I had a lot of work ahead of me. I wanted to try and get as much water out of the basement as possible to avoid damage. So I took on the laborious process of bailing out the basement bucket by bucket— up the stairs, out the front door, dumping it, and going back down the stairs to repeat the procedure. To lessen how many times

I had to climb the stairs, I brought down trash cans and filled them, hoping to dump them once the sump was working again. I spent hours bailing and going up and down the stairs to dump the buckets.

Kris was facing a similar situation at her house, except she was able to keep ahead of the basement flooding with her bucket bailing. Once we all realized the power was not coming on anytime soon, Gary, her fiancé at the time, took his generator to her house. Once the generator warmed up her house and emptied her sump, they both were kind enough to come to my house and use the generator to pump out my basement. I was exhausted, cranky, and felt ready to lose my cool.

Gary brought me out of my negative funk, though. He flipped the tables for me by pointing out that although my basement had flooded, everything I had in the basement was in plastic tubs, and nothing was ruined by the water. How fortunate! In the midst of the bailing, all I could focus on was the water, not that I hadn't actually lost anything. I never took a moment to look at the bigger picture and realize I was actually lucky. From that moment on, I felt a sense of peace with the whole negative situation.

After hooking up the generator, we headed upstairs. Gary, Kris, and I had a chance to visit and catch up while the water was being pumped from the basement. Gary even figured out how to turn on the fireplace manually for me. It was actually relaxing to be chatting by the fireplace and a room lit by candles. Despite the day's events, we all had a pleasant and peaceful time together. Moments like those are ones you never forget for the rest of your life.

Once the water was pumped out, and Gary was about to head home, he said he had something to tell me but didn't want to upset me. Yet, he wanted to make sure

I knew this information just in case of another power outage. He proceeded to tell me that I had been dumping the bailed water right along the foundation of the house. So the bailed water (hundreds of buckets' worth) was likely feeding right back into the sump in the basement. In other words, I had been bailing the same water over and over again.

I could have been mad or frustrated, or even just cried after hours of bailing, but all we could do was laugh. We still laugh to this day about that incident. It wasn't a situation that I would want to relive, but you know what? With good friends and a positive attitude, you can get through just about anything. Friends have a way of bringing you a sense of peace in negative moments.

In Jeanie's stories, there was no way anyone could stop the weather related negativity. As we all know, Mother Nature has a mind of her own. However, with the help of fun stories, support of coworkers and friends, there is a way to find some peace in the moments you may be facing.

In the next story, Kris shares an incident that illustrates a few more ways to find peace in a moment. Sometimes these feelings of peace hit you when you're not expecting them. It's important to try and be aware of what's happening and use that glimmer of peace to help deal with the moment.

The Chainsaw

By Kris

In March of 2012, Western New York had the warmest March on record. We had brilliant, sunny days and eighty-degree temperatures. It was absolutely perfect, for most people anyway. For me, I was struggling emotionally because my mother had just passed away after a brief illness. I was trying to get by moment by moment. I had a low patience level, no energy to be with the kids, and no interest in much of anything. I had lost my decision making ability, my creativity, and my positive energy. It had been three weeks since my mother died and my husband was hoping a change of scenery might help perk me up a bit. He suggested that we go away for the weekend.

His parents have a house in a town about an hour south of where we live. We spend a lot of time there in the winter because it's very close to the ski area we like. There's a lot of land, no close neighbors, and a beautiful deck that's perfect for sitting out on and reading books. Gary knows reading is one of my favorite pastimes. He said, and I quote him directly, "C'mon, we'll go down there for the weekend, relax, and you can find lots of reading time on the deck!" Reluctantly I agreed, but I figured getting out would be good for me.

On Saturday morning we actually were able to go

skiing. What a glorious morning— sunny and sixty-five degrees. Gary even had his shorts on! It doesn't get better than that for him. It was the perfect morning. I felt my spirits lift with every run down the hill. There is something so peaceful about skiing down a hill with the wind in your face and the sun shining down on you. It's as if all of your cares and worries just disappear.

We headed home around lunch time. I was feeling the best I had felt in weeks. I could still feel a fog around me, but I had hope that things were going to get better. After lunch, rather than sitting and reading a book, we started to do some yard work. After all, it was so pleasant out, and it felt good to do some manual labor.

The town public works department had recently come by and cut some dead limbs off of the trees and even a large, dead tree in front of the house. They had left some large branches, so we pulled them into the driveway. Gary got out his chainsaw and began cutting them up. When that was done, there were a few low branches hanging down over the driveway. He violated a chainsaw safety rule and reached up over his head to cut the branches down. Those branches were very thorny. So imagine how you would feel if you looked up and saw a branch falling toward you, rather than away from you, as you would have expected. Gary took a step back and his right leg slid about a foot down a steep embankment. As he did that, his left leg came up and the chainsaw (as it was winding down) caught his knee.

At first, I couldn't tell what had happened. I was behind Gary, about one hundred feet away. I saw him slip down the bank, and immediately heard the chainsaw go off. My first thought was that he had twisted his ankle. But then I heard his voice, soft and calm, almost oddly calm.

"Can you get me a towel? I'm bleeding."

"How bad?" I asked.

"I am not sure yet," he replied.

I ran in and got a towel. When I came out, I realized his knee was definitely in need of stitches. However, through this whole thing, Gary remained calm and positive. He said things like, "Maybe I don't need stitches. It'll be okay. Let's just see how it is."

The next day, I found out he was saying all of those things because he was embarrassed about what had happened. Embarrassed that he hadn't worn safety gear. Embarrassed that he cut a branch over his head. He didn't want people to find out he had been the "s" word. (Note: The "s" word originated from the "Meatball Frenzy" story later on in this book and means stupid.)

But after a phone call with our doctor, it was decided Gary needed to get to the closest hospital. The doctor didn't want him driving the hour back to Buffalo. The wound needed to be cleaned out as soon as possible to avoid infection. So, Gary and his mom went off to the hospital. I stayed back with the kids. It was such a hard thing, watching Gary and his mom pull out of the driveway, but I knew the kids needed me.

Both kids saw the accident and the blood after. They knew what was going on. When they heard Daddy was going to the hospital, my eldest asked, "Now will Daddy die just like Grandma, because he's going to the hospital?"

Wow! At that moment everything became clear to me. It snapped me back into reality and out of the fog I was in since my mom's passing. I took both kids in my arms and gave them the biggest hug ever. I told them, and I firmly believed it myself, "Daddy will be okay. He has a great angel, Grandma, who is with him right now, helping him."

A few hours went by and I finally heard from Gary.

His leg had been cleaned up and he was waiting to get stitches. Luckily, he did not cut any bone or muscles. What a relief! I could feel the tears fall down my face as he told me the good news. He was at a small hospital, and there was another emergency the staff was tending to, so he was just waiting.

He was lying on a table, with his wound wide open and a blue sheet over it. He couldn't move and was quite uncomfortable. Instead of complaining and telling me how bad it was, he told me he was "thankful he just had a chainsaw cut." Just a chainsaw cut? The outcome could have been so awful for him, and he was telling me he was lucky? I was thinking he must be on pain medication, or he had lost a lot of blood. Then he continued:

"I may be uncomfortable now, but I'm going to walk in a few weeks. The woman in the room next to me is having a heart attack and fighting for her life. The emergency helicopter is involved in another case, and the next ambulance from Buffalo is about forty-five minutes out. This hospital is not equipped to deal with her, so there is a chance she won't make it. I'll take my cut leg."

I really do believe this man is an angel sent here to keep me on track. Somehow, he finds the positive in everything and has a belief that doesn't waiver.

"It'll work out," he said. That outlook brought a wave of peace over me, and from the tone of his voice, I knew he had found his peace, too.

Gary came home from the hospital about six hours, twenty-five stitches, and two pain pills after the incident. I was so happy to see him! His leg was bandaged, he was limping, and it was obvious he was in pain. One of the first things he said to me was, "How are you?" From the tone of his voice, I knew he understood how worried I had been about him. He also knew how I had been feeling about my mom, and this stress could have been the straw that made me snap. Instead, it opened my eyes. Deep down I knew that everything would be okay.

Bad things happen to us all, but it's how you react to the situation that determines the overall experience. Yes, Gary had been injured. Yet none of us yelled at him or questioned why he didn't wear his safety gear. It wouldn't have helped the situation. We were all just so appreciative (yes, appreciative is the right word here) that it wasn't worse. That gratitude brought us a sense of peace that everything was going to be okay.

❀ ❀ ❀ ❀ ❀ ❀

Every person will have to find what works best for him or her to bring them peace. It's such a personal thing and differs greatly from person to person. Some people like loud music to calm them while others like soft, classical music. Some people work out or go for a long run while others prefer yoga or meditating. One person may find peace with a rainy day while another person may find that a rainy day makes them feel depressed. The most important thing to do is to listen to yourself. Listen to your mind, your body, and your heart. You'll know what feels best for you and what works to help you find peace. Take a deep breath, pause, and listen to your inner voice.

We hope none of you ever are faced with the situation Kris is about to relate to you. It's a story she has only shared with a few people because it still breaks her heart when she thinks about it. However, when we were working on this book, she thought this story was a perfect example of how a stranger helped her find peace during a tense and emotional situation. Even in the worst possible negative moments there are ways to find a minute of peace. And sometimes a minute is all you need to gather your thoughts and move forward.

The Overlook

By Kris

It was a beautiful sunny day, and Gary and I were on our way home from an out-of-state camping trip. It had been a wonderful weekend, and we decided to take one last break for lunch. We stopped at a state park and picked a scenic spot overlooking a valley for our picnic. We were enjoying each other's company and laughing about all the good moments of the trip. Suddenly, we were jarred out of our bliss by a woman screaming "No!"

We immediately noticed that there was a woman standing dangerously close to the edge of the overlook. We assumed she must have climbed the small fence that was there, but we were puzzled as to why she would do that. Three people were standing opposite of her on the "right" side of the fence and they looked extremely anxious.

As we made our way over to the area, another man came running by and yelled to us, "She's going to jump! Do you have any rope?" Since we had just been camping, we had plenty of rope in the truck. Gary and the man ran to get the rope while I continued towards the commotion.

As I got within ten feet, the woman looked back at what I found out later was her family and said, "There is a letter in my desk drawer." Then, she jumped. It was the most horrific thing I had ever seen in my life. To this day, I have never experienced anything even close to that.

There are no words to describe the emotions I was feeling. I know they were all negative, but it was like nothing I had ever felt before. I stood there in disbelief. I had no idea what to do. I couldn't move a single body part. I was so shocked. My mind went blank. Before I knew what was going on, Gary had returned with rope, and there were now several men with him. They secured Gary with the rope and lowered him partially down the overhang. Everyone was hoping that maybe this woman got hung up in a tree, and they could save her.

That was not the case. When she jumped, she cleared the overhang where they had lowered Gary. She fell about two hundred feet. She must have died instantly. I was standing in the middle of her family members shaking like I had never shaken before. There were three of them. It turned out she had invited her brother, his wife, and their cousin to join her on a hike in the park that day. I was standing next to her brother, and he told me he figured she didn't want to be alone when she died.

He and I both had tears running down our cheeks. We watched his wife and cousin embrace and cry, too. It was a surreal moment. Everything was happening in slow motion. My stomach hurt. I couldn't think straight, and I couldn't process what was happening.

Then, the brother turned to me and said, "You know, she had a particularly aggressive form of cancer. She was so tired of fighting it. She believed we treat our animals at the end of their life more decently than we treat humans. She never discussed her plans with me, but I am guessing she wanted a way out from this. I hope she is in a better place now. The agony and wait is over."

I can't tell you that I understand or support what this woman did. What I can tell you, though, is that her brother's words brought me peace at that moment. As soon as he finished talking, I felt like I could breathe again. My rational thoughts emerged and I kicked into react mode. I made sure someone had called the police. When the police arrived, I met them and brought them to the family. I checked on the family to see if they wanted anything to drink. Just five minutes prior, I couldn't even move my feet. Now here I was, like a mother hen running around trying to help where I could.

In hindsight, it seems crazy that I was able to find peace in the midst of what had just occurred. But in those few minutes of clarity, when I was able to absorb why the negative situation may have occurred, I was able to breathe, calm myself, and react rationally. It was a horrible moment that I will never forget for the rest of my life. The situation was out of my control, and there was nothing I could do to flip the tables. I only hope that woman found her own peace somewhere.

As a follow-up to this story, about six months after the incident, Gary and I decided to return to the overlook. We wanted to spend some time there so we could remember the spot in a more positive light. We thought if we went back and shared new memories, maybe those horrific memories wouldn't be quite so vivid.

We packed a lunch and headed to our spot. As we approached the area, there was a man sitting on the bench. He was very calm, and his face looked peaceful. As I got closer to him, I realized it was the woman's brother. I never found out his name or where he was from. I have no idea how many times he had returned to that spot. But for us to be there at the same time as him, I figured it was some kind of sign. A sign telling us to believe that the woman found her peace. We didn't stop to talk to the man. We didn't want to rehash how we knew him. We just found our own spot, sat down, and gazed out at the overlook in peace.

❀ ❀ ❀ ❀ ❀ ❀

Kris often thinks back on that day and that moment of peace. At that minute, she didn't feel good about what was going on around her, but she was able to catch her breath and clear her mind for a minute. In essence, it gave her time to "pause."

Every day is made up of many moments and opportunities for positive or negative outcomes. There are so many ways to find peace in the negative moments. How do you find your second to pause and find peace in moments?

In her adult years, Kris has always felt strongly that "everything happens for a reason." She talks about it in the next story, and will show you how that belief brings her peace in negative moments and helps her continue to "nip it in the butt!"

Everything Happens for a Reason

By Kris

Writing this book has given me a lot of time to reflect on my core values and beliefs. One of my core strengths that I draw upon all the time is my belief that "everything happens for a reason." I have been trying to determine when I formed that belief. Was it as a child, teenager, in college, or since I have been an adult?

I have memories from my childhood of my mom always laughing when something didn't quite turn out the way she had planned. Like the time she baked a loaf of zucchini bread. She was cutting it and hit something hard. After further investigation, she realized there was something inside the loaf. She took the loaf apart, and her first words after discovering a spoon in it were "Oh, that's where the mixing spoon went."

There was not a word about how all the work to make a loaf of bread was essentially a waste of time. It was honestly funny to her and not a big deal. Who knows, maybe she was asking herself *Does it really matter?*

I remember one time when the dog took her glasses off the table and ran into the backyard whipping them around. The dog had a blast. I was all prepared to try and corner the dog (a 90-pound Labrador/German shepherd mix), but she turned to me and said, "I needed a new pair anyway." She didn't say anything like how bad the dog was or what she was going to do until she got a new pair. She just laughed and let the dog enjoy the moment.

I was an overachiever during my high school years. My parents did not put pressure on me to get good grades, but they did instill a value of always working to your potential and giving it your best shot. I had a 4.0 average for over two years. When I got my first B, I was devastated. I came home from school and there was a huge cake waiting for me. On it was written "Congratulations Kris on Your B." Mom was celebrating my success, showing me I was human. She didn't give me any pep talk about how if I had studied harder, I would have received an A. She told me this B was great because it took the pressure off me of maintaining a 4.0 average. She provided me with a fresh angle on that situation.

When I got cut from the softball team, my mom didn't tell me she was sorry. Her response was, "Look on the bright side, now we don't have to cancel our trip to the Adirondacks due to softball games." She always had a unique perspective on the curve balls that life throws at you. So I think my belief that "everything happens for a reason" started as a child. Having such a value grows stronger with every moment in your life that it's applied.

From my years in college, I have a memory of being disappointed that I didn't get in a certain class that I really wanted. I heard the professor was great and exciting, and "everyone" was taking the class. It turned out the class I did get into would forever change my life. The professor was incredible, and I enjoyed it so much that I changed my major from psychology to computer science.

Three years later, that same professor helped me get my first job out of college. I had already secured a job in

Annapolis, Maryland. I was excited about the job and moving in with a close college friend, but my heart wasn't in it. My family lived near Buffalo, and I didn't want to leave them.

During finals, this professor stopped by while I was studying and said, "I think what I'm about to say will change your life in a major way." He told me a local company was hiring, and I, along with five others from our graduating class, could be interviewed for the position. I went on the interview, and as it turned out I got the job. The company made me an offer two days before I was to leave for Annapolis. That day was one of the happiest of my life. I really believed I was following my heart to stay near my family and I often wonder what would have happened had I been placed in the class I "really" wanted. Where would I have ended up?

I bought my first house a few years after I finished college. My dear friend and cousin came in from out of town to spend the night. I was so excited that she was going to be in my home and for us to have a fabulous girls' weekend. We woke up the first morning to find ants. Not just a few ants, but hundreds of ants all over the kitchen! I remember my first thought was that this was going to ruin our visit. But within seconds, the core value woke up and I tried focusing on believing it was happening for a reason. I have to admit, it sure isn't easy when you have bugs running all over your counter tops and floors. There were so many ants that it looked like they were invading and would eat me and Keri alive!

As I always did when I lived in that house, I called my dad for help. He said, "A lot of times where there are ants, there is water." Then, he came over and found a leak in my bathroom wall that was going down to the first floor. If not for the ants, I probably would have had severe water damage. Dad cut a hole in my wall, fixed the leak, and after a few bottles of ant spray, all was well. Instead of making some homemade meals for Keri, we had some great meals and conversations out at restaurants. Thank you ants!

Many years later, I was thirty-five weeks pregnant with my first child and still working fifty hours a week. I knew I needed to slow down, but there was so much I wanted to get done at work before my maternity leave. I ended up having some complications and the doctor pulled me out of work. I was so upset. I hadn't finished all my transition plans and training. I had all sorts of loose ends to tie up.

I vividly remember sitting in the doctor's office and asking "Why is this happening to me?" She answered, "It's simple, this is happening because you aren't slowing down. Your body needs to slow down. So you had a little bump in the road. You are so lucky. You and the baby are perfectly healthy. But your body is telling you to slow down. That's why this is happening and that's why I'm making you stop work."

That doctor provided me with a new perspective very quickly! I also learned some valuable things during that time. Nothing is more important than your family, and if you truly listen to your body, it sure has a lot to tell you.

In early 2012, I was driving to work with my almost three-year-old in the car. As always, I was a bit on the edgy side. It never ceases to amaze me how hectic mornings at home can be with two children. No matter how much I plan and do the night before, mornings turn into a chaotic frenzy of missing shoes, toothpaste dripped shirts, and tantrums about having hair brushed. Trying to pack up and get out of the house with a toddler takes as much energy and patience as running a marathon.

We were driving on a road with a speed limit of forty-five miles per hour. There was a gray van in front of me going thirty miles an hour. He or she was just put-zing along as if they didn't have a care in the world. I could feel my blood pressure rise, but I kept repeating in my head, *There is a reason I need to go slowly.* I continued to take deep breaths to stay calm.

We approached a large intersection and the traffic light was green. The van slowed down to twenty miles per hour, and it was clear we would not make it through that light. Yet, when the light turned yellow, the van's driver gunned the engine and went racing through light, which had turned red.

I don't think even Gandhi could have stayed peaceful with that one. I smacked the steering wheel with my hands and I yelled out loud, "Are you kidding me?" I figured it was probably some kids screwing around.

Of course I startled my little one, and from the back seat she wanted to know, "Momma, what's so funny? Who is kidding you?" Her comment immediately cut through my frustration, and I laughed with her. I took a deep breath while sitting at the red light and thought, *Thank you, gray van driver, for letting me have that giggle with my Sara.* My spirit lifted, and I was able to forget the whole incident until I went two more miles down the road.

It was then that traffic stalled again, and I could tell there was some kind of commotion ahead of us. I slowed down, and as we approached the congestion, I saw a deer had been hit and was lying in the middle of the road. Guess which car was pulled over to the side? The gray van! If I hadn't been forced to stop at the red light, would I have been involved in the accident, too? There is no way of knowing for sure, but incidents like this really make me stop and reflect that everything truly happens for a reason.

Writing this book has helped me realize that this core value is not one that got switched on or off at any one moment in time. It's a type of faith that I have been surrounded with and have worked on building for years. I have trust in it and I strive to implement it moment by moment in my life. Sometimes I may become aware of the reason something happened in that moment, or days, months, or even years later, or maybe never. But having this core belief has helped me find peace through small as well as life changing moments.

I understand that this may be hard for some people to embrace. A similar value is one my mother-in-law recites on a regular basis: "Something good comes out of everything." It's a similar mantra but maybe not so "heavy" or definitive. And her belief may be easier to apply to life changing events.

In February of 2009, Flight 3407 crashed on its approach to the Buffalo airport. My company lost four outstanding workers that day and Gary and I lost four friends. To this day, I have yet to find a connection to, "everything happens for a reason." In my heart of hearts, though, I truly believe there must be a reason for it. I may never know until I meet up with these delightful souls in heaven, but I keep believing.

In the meantime, I have witnessed something good come out of the tragedy. Families have grown closer, new friendships have been made, and the families of Flight 3407 helped changed legislation that will make it safer for all of us to fly. This little bit of good will never fill the emptiness any of us feel. However, for me, I feel a little bit of peace knowing that something good did come out of losing these four remarkable men.

❀ ❀ ❀ ❀ ❀ ❀

Finding peace within will be a personal journey in each negative moment you face. The tools you use may differ with each type of negative moment you encounter, too. One way to find peace in negative moments is to lean on the strength of your friends. In the following story, Jeanie tells us how a friend helped her deal with a negative moment.

Christmas Cootie Challenge

By Jeanie

My brother-in-law's family plays a game called Cootie. The object of the game is extraordinarily simple: do not get stuck with the cootie. The cootie is a small, plastic bug that looks like one of those from the children's board game Cootie. It is multicolored, about three inches long, and about one inch wide.

My sister and brother-in-law have had a lot of fun playing this game with his family. Their cootie has traveled all over the world, since the family is spread out across the globe. At holidays they are all together, and when it's time to leave, you never know who may end up with the cootie in a suitcase or clothing item or even in a Christmas present. Most of the time you do not even know you have the cootie until you get home and begin to unpack.

This game was so popular with my extended family that I decided to buy a cootie for myself and start the tradition with my friends in Western New York. The Cootie game, as we play it, starts with the cootie being "given" to someone without them knowing. When you get stuck with the cootie, the goal is to get rid of it by "giving" it to someone else.

You can hide the cootie in their house, leave it in

their luggage, or maybe place it in the pocket of their jacket. The ways to transfer the cootie are only limited by your imagination. There is one main rule: In order to have a successful transfer of the cootie, the unsuspecting receiver of the cootie must not discover the cootie while the giver of the cootie is present. If the cootie is discovered, it is immediately returned to the giver.

To start the game, my first cootie exchange was at a party at Kris and Gary's house. It was an easy transfer. I was able to hide the cootie behind a book on their book shelf. After all, at this point, they didn't even know they were about to become part of the Western New York version of the "Cootie" game. After the party, I sent an e-mail out to the group of friends and introduced everyone to this game. Kris and Gary were the first victims who had to figure out a way to get rid of the cootie by giving it to someone in the group. Little did I know I would create a frenzy.

My group of friends is a gang of jokesters and pranksters. Many of them have engineering backgrounds and live for a challenge. They loved the idea behind the Cootie game, and the cootie has been hidden in some ingenuous places.

Once I hid the cootie in the wall of Kris and Gary's unfinished house. Luckily, they found the cootie before the dry wall was installed. Another time it was hidden in a partially eaten bag of potato chips that someone took home after a party. Last year the cootie was even buried in a container of hot chocolate that was given as a Christmas present. Yet, my favorite transfer was the time Gary taped the cootie to the bumper of a car.

The game has made us all very suspicious of each other when we leave a gathering. Everyone checks their pockets, empties all packages, and always keeps their car doors locked. It's a fun game that has been going on for more than ten years, but it does tend to raise our guard at the end of an event together.

One annual event that is prime for a cootie exchange is our group's Christmas party. One particular year, I made a rookie cootie mistake when I arrived at the party—I left my car unlocked. The party ended at about midnight, and it was a very cold December night. I remotely started my car and waited inside the house for it to warm up. I thoroughly searched all my belongings to make sure the cootie had not been slipped into my purse or coat pockets. I gathered my things and went out to the car.

I got in and happened to look in the center console, and there sat the cootie. I jumped out of the car and ran to the house to playfully scold Bob, the host of the party, for trying to give me the cootie. Unfortunately, in my haste, I had thrown my keys on the passenger seat. And then out of habit, I locked the car doors as I was jumping out of the car. Right as I slammed the car door, I realized what had happened.

I was now locked out of my car at midnight on a freezing December night in Western New York. Instead of laughing about it, my first thoughts immediately were negative. *How am I going to get someone to come and unlock my car at this hour?* It was late, and I needed to get home to my dogs. I lived about forty-five minutes away from where the party was held. I was fretting more and more with every step to Bob's front door.

When I knocked on the front door, Bob wouldn't open the door for me at first. He thought it was a ploy to give the cootie back to him. As I said before, although we all love each other dearly, the cootie transfers have been creative and we have tried almost anything to dump the cootie off on someone else.

After a few minutes of asking Bob to open his door, I think my exasperated voice finally convinced him I was serious about locking my keys in my car. When he finally let me in the house and I told him what happened, he found the whole situation rather comical. Up to this point, the cootie had never made any of us lock our keys in a car. I still was not laughing about the situation. I was angry and frustrated with myself for being so irrational, and I was worried about my dogs being left home alone for so many hours.

Bob saw I was having a moment and offered to call the tow truck driver for me. If he had made me do the calling, I probably would have started crying. As I write this, I am thinking to myself, *Why on earth did I get so spun up? It really wasn't a big deal.* That's the thing with this negativity stuff: sometimes it just hits you. Sometimes it's in situations that really aren't that bad. But the thing is, sometimes it will nip you despite the reality of the situation. This was one of those moments. Even though I was safe and with a friend, and had help on the way, all I could focus on was the negative. It was cold, and I had done a dumb thing!

While we waited for the tow truck, Bob continued with "Bobspective" to try and make me feel better. He joked and reminded me it was really no big deal that I locked myself out of the car. He seemed determined to help me make peace with what I had done.

It worked well enough. By the time the tow truck arrived and the driver unlocked my car, I was feeling better and able to drive home. And now when we talk about that night, I'm able to laugh with everyone else about how the originator of the cootie game locked herself out of her car all because a small, plastic toy was in the console!

❀ ❀ ❀ ❀ ❀ ❀

In the cootie situation, Jeanie perceived everything that was happening as negative, and she felt there was nothing that could change it. Her view of the moment caused her to feel bad for herself and become frustrated. The feelings may not have been rational, but they were what she was feeling.

This will happen to each of us at some time in our lives. Hopefully, when you go through moments like this, you will have a good friend at your side who understands we all get nipped from time to time, and who will call the tow truck for you. Bob's support and attitude helped Jeanie find a little bit of peace in the moment. It may not have flipped her tables or nipped the negativity entirely in the butt, however, it was enough peace to settle her thoughts a bit and allow her to drive home safely.

Never underestimate that sense of peace you can provide to a friend, family member or significant other. In the next story, with a hug and a few sentences, Kris was able to help Gary find a sliver of peace in a moment where he was feeling disappointed, vulnerable, and violated.

The Lost Wallet

By Kris

My husband Gary is a perfectionist when it comes to gift shopping. He wants to make sure he buys the ideal gift for the lucky recipient. When you receive a gift from him (even if it's a box of chocolates), you can rest assured knowing that he has analyzed it from every angle to make sure it's perfect for you. He is one of the most thoughtful gift buyers I have ever met. Every December I so look forward to Christmas morning to see what new treasures he has found for me.

Gary traditionally waits until the December calendar is in the twenties before he begins to think about Christmas shopping. He says he likes the pressure because it will force him to make a decision. If he started in November like I do, I can only imagine the amount of research he would complete on that candle his mom asked for or the box of chocolates for an aunt.

One year, on December 23rd, Gary took an afternoon off work to start his shopping adventure. He headed to a large department store and spent the afternoon selecting and choosing multiple gifts for me and his family. He had a large basket of items and proceeded to the checkout. As he reached into his pocket, he found his wallet was missing. He instantly knew what had happened. Someone had bumped into him in an aisle and he remembered it being an awkward moment. As he reflected, Gary realized his wallet had been pickpocketed.

Imagine the anger and frustration he felt. After all of his hard work to earn that money and then select the perfect gifts he wouldn't be able to purchase. That afternoon he had withdrawn his Christmas spending money from an ATM, and now it was all gone.

When Gary walked in the house that day, I knew something was terribly wrong. He had such a sad look on his face. All he said was, "Christmas is over."

After he told me what had happened, all I did was hug him and tell him that "all I needed for Christmas was him, safe and home with me."

Those words and that hug provided Gary a little bit of peace in the moment. It didn't flip the tables or nip the negativity. When someone steals from you, it's hard to understand why, and it's hard not to feel negative about it. However, you can try and find some peace in the moment and learn to forgive over time.

On Christmas Eve, Gary used our credit card to go shopping and buy some presents. He wasn't much in the spirit, but he gave it his best attempt. Christmas was still perfect that year because we had each other and our families with which to celebrate.

Then, on December 27th, Gary received an envelope in the mail. It was all of the contents of his wallet, except the cash. We have no idea who mailed it to us, but at least he got his pictures back, along with some other personal items in his wallet. Ironically, even though the money was not returned, Gary felt more peaceful about the situation and was able to let go of the negativity.

You never know how you may find peace in a moment. Sometimes it may be very difficult, but in smaller moments like these, we believe there is always a way. The more you work on having an overall positive attitude about life, the easier finding peace will become when you are in a negative moment that you cannot nip.

When you change your thought process, look at situations differently, or understand what helps you find peace, you will feel a shift in your life. Slowly you will notice that you feel different once a day, and that will turn into a few times a day, which will eventually become most of the day. A positive outlook on life makes you feel happier, gives you more energy, and helps build lasting relationships with people who continue to "build you up."

Making your life happier will help you through less happy moments. You will be able to dig deep and find peace to help you deal with anything life throws at you. A positive attitude becomes a life changing decision that affects you in so many ways. What kind of attitude do you have? Are you happy with it? If not, make a decision now to change. Be more positive and be happier!

Chapter 7

Leave It

Walk Away from Negativity

The previous chapters have provided some hints on how to nip negativity in the butt and flip the tables on a situation. In reality, sometimes those techniques won't work, and you just have to get yourself out of the moment. You may have to walk away or rely on someone else to get you out of the moment. Too often self-help books paint a rosy picture by telling you if you follow a certain amount of steps, your life will be perfect, and you will forever be happy. We are positive and optimistic people, but even we know it doesn't work that way all the time. Occasionally life throws curve balls at you, and you may not be able to change the moment in any way.

Coaching you to get out of a negative situation doesn't mean giving up on it altogether. Look at what's happening in your moment and try to change it, but if that isn't working, it's okay to walk away. Actually, it's more than okay. In some cases it may be the healthiest thing for you to do.

In the first story, Jeanie shares a personal situation where negativity from a friend was bothering her. Eventually, she decided it was best to let it go, move on, and proceed forward with a decision despite her friend's advice. By letting it go, she got out of the moment and saw the big picture more clearly.

Joining the Marine Corps

By Jeanie

I've been thinking a lot lately about why I wanted to write this book with Kris. The most compelling reason is that she asked, and I would do just about anything for her and her husband Gary. They have been good friends to me through the years, and I hope I have been a good friend to them, as well.

The problem with my side of writing this book is history, or actually the lack of history. I'll be honest; I had never even heard of positive energy until I met Kris. I didn't characterize people as positive or negative, and never took much notice of how people can subtly change the mood of everyone in a room. So while Kris has spent a lifetime developing her sense of positive and negative energy, I am a novice at this art. Yet, since meeting Kris, I have become so much more attuned to how someone can come into a room and simply suck the life out of you.

Here's an example. Many, many years ago, I was working and going to school part-time, not sure where my life was going to take me and not feeling passionate about any one thing. Then on a whim, I went to a military recruiting office and was instantly enamored with the idea of joining the Marine Corps. I spent some time thinking about it, going through all the options, and making sure I understood the commitment I was making. After giving it a lot of thought and doing a lot of research, I decided I wanted to join the Marine Corps. I called my good friend Glen and told him about my visit to the recruiter. I reviewed my research with him and informed him of my decision. I was very excited as I told him about the opportunities with the Marines.

When I shared the news with Glen, he was less than supportive. His words implied that this was just another one of my impulsive ideas and that I would never become a Marine. He didn't feel I was serious or committed to the idea. He said I should continue to go to school until something ignited my passion. Pow! With that one remark, he drained all of the positive energy and enthusiasm from me. I was decidedly down. I started second-guessing whether I should even move forward with joining the Marines. And I hadn't even realized he had used the "should" word with me. It truly is astonishing how that word can deflate someone's bubble.

That night I just kept thinking about my friend's words and seriously doubting what I was thinking. His opinion was causing much turmoil for me. Finally, I decided the heck with it. Even if it turned out to be another impulse, it would serve to move my life forward in a new direction. So I went to the recruiter and joined the Marine Corps. It was one of the best decisions of my life. I spent four years serving my country as a United States Marine and enjoyed every minute of it!

In this example, you can see how my friend's remark had an impact on me. He probably never gave it much thought and will never realize how much it bothered me. In this situation, I couldn't change his belief about my decision. Instead, I had to let it go and get out of the moment. I pressed ahead with what I had planned to do and worked hard to keep a positive attitude about joining the Marines. I will be honest- I did worry a little about what he thought. But in the end, I made the decision for me.

Sometimes it's difficult for me to stop in the moment and adjust. Yet even adjusting a day or two later helps and still allows me to prevent a potentially negative comment from adversely affecting me long term. It has taken me awhile to learn to recognize these people and situations. As I've said, I still work on how I handle them. We're always going to encounter negativity in life. We can't control it, but we can control how we let it affect us. That's why I'm coauthoring this book. I don't have some incredible knowledge to share, some secret of the universe, but I am living proof that the knowledge and suggestions Kris shared with me are real and have positively impacted my life. My life is more positive and I am happier. If, working with Kris, we can change just one more person's life, then we have accomplished our original goal.

Once Jeanie let the negative feelings go, she was able to move forward and concentrate on what was best for her life. Moving past negative feelings can be a hard thing to do, especially when making life decisions. Many of us care deeply about how our friends view us. When you are going through life, it feels good when your friends understand and are supportive of your life choices. Try and become more aware of how you feel when you are interacting with your friends and family. Are you walking away feeling more upbeat and energized, or are your negative vibe indicators kicked up a notch?

Depending on your answer, you may need to take some action. In Jeanie's case, she was able just to let it go and make the choice that she determined was best for her. Some of you may not be in a position to do that. In those cases, we believe open communication with your family and friends is an excellent option. Rather than letting negative feelings sit and fester, have a talk with your friend and let him or her know how you are feeling. Explain the specific actions or words that you perceived caused a negative situation. With an open dialog, hopefully you will be able to work through the issue and avoid negative encounters like this in the future.

In the next story, Kris gets out of a negative moment quite differently than how Jeanie got out of hers. It only took Kris a few minutes to reflect and see how the moment was affecting her and her potential reactions. In both cases, we nipped the negativity in the butt and we didn't let ourselves get caught in a downward negative spiral for long. We both walked away from our situations feeling better.

Biting My Tongue

By Kris

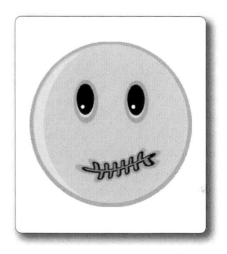

As you have learned from a few stories, 2012 was a turbulent year for me. One of the principal factors contributing to this turbulence was that my employer implemented its third workforce reduction in three years. That type of change creates a lot of upheaval and uneasiness with employees. Luckily I retained my job, but it certainly was a challenging environment for months after the third round of employees were let go.

From my experience, the feelings of an employee remaining at a company after a workforce reduction can include sadness, guilt, and anxiety. Then, on top of all those emotions, in most cases, the people who are left have to take on new roles and responsibilities to cover the work of the people who were let go. This normally results in a heavier workload and, ultimately, if not managed properly, can add to the employee's stress.

In my case, I had taken on additional work and had been pushed to the max for about six months. I always smiled, though, and I did my best to never take my stress out on anyone else. After all, we were in the same boat, and everyone was super busy. We were all trying to understand our new roles and responsibilities, and I felt it was only fair to have patience with everyone.

Another group in the company had just received a special project from management outside of our local office. The project was in my area of expertise, so although I had no free time, I offered to help and facilitate the team assigned. On the day the team met to develop an action plan to support the execution of the project, one individual was antagonistic and pushed back on everything we were doing. She made it clear that this project was a waste of her time, and she had better things to do. In all honesty that may have been the case, but I didn't make the assignment nor did I set the deadline. I truly was just trying to help and facilitate its success.

I could tell by her body language and tone that she was upset. So I did my best to try and convince her that what we were doing was important, but she made it difficult to remain positive. Even her boss added some fuel to the fire by arguing with me about the worthiness of the assignment. Again, I reminded them that this project wasn't my idea; someone higher up thought it was necessary and I was just helping out because I had some expertise in the area.

The antagonistic individual proceeded to use some words that implied what I was doing did not add value to the group, nor to the company in general. As soon as she made it personal, my blood boiled, and my face turned as red as a fire engine. For me this was highly unusual. I don't get mad often. I almost never feel anger as I did on that day. I normally pull myself out of moments before my emotions reach that level.

My first instinct was to snap and tell her I was done helping and they were on their own. At that moment I did not care if they succeeded or not. I don't typically feel ambivalent, especially in a work environment. I'm normally a true team player that pitches in wherever the company needs me. However, at the time, I was so angry I understood what the expression "seeing red" meant, and I truly wanted to tell this woman she was on her own.

I took a deep breath and reflected for a second. I knew my negative indicators were being set off in a major way. I had to continue to pause and take a few moments for myself. Everyone in the room understood that this individual had crossed a line. It was so silent in the room, you literally could have heard a piece of hay drop (yes, another "ism").

All eyes were on me, and I knew I had to say something. Here is how I responded: "I'm going to sit here, bite my tongue, and cool down. You have made me very angry, and I don't want to say something I will regret."

I was blunt and straight to the point, but it was what I had to do to get out of that negative moment. I wasn't feeling very rational. Taking me out of the moment in that manner did something that actually surprised me— it took everyone else out of the moment as well!

I quickly found out that the antagonistic individual did not mean to make me angry. She went on to explain she was under a lot of stress, had some important deadlines to meet, and felt she wasn't getting the support she needed from others in the organization. She had a deadline that day, and it truly was more important than what we were working on. Her boss then followed up by letting me know he sincerely did appreciate the help and would work on the issues.

What a difference pausing for a moment truly makes. Who knew taking myself out of that moment would immediately nip the negativity in the butt and flip the tables for good. Over the following weeks, the team and I met and completed the project on time and successfully.

I continue to learn about the power of this moment

by moment stuff every day, too, and I am so grateful for the opportunity to have a part in writing this book. I am focusing more on my attitude, the situations I encounter, and my reactions. This attention is helping me to improve my experience of moments each and every day.

❀ ❀ ❀ ❀ ❀ ❀

In both of the previous stories, we were able to successfully get out of the negative moment. We used different techniques, but each was effective. In some cases, you may not be able to get out of the moment yourself. That is when you lean on other people if you have to, especially if it's a potential safety issue, as in the next story. The individual in that story knew when a situation was out of her hands, and she needed to call for reinforcements. She paid attention to what was happening around her, how she was feeling, and how others were reacting. That's how she knew she needed help.

Call in the Troops

By Kris

As I mentioned in a previous story, during an appointment for a blood draw, I met a technician whose mantra in life was "nothing good comes from being negative." After talking with her for about twenty minutes, I perceived her to be a warm and wise woman. She was one of those people who draws you in as they talk, and has an air about them that is uplifting.

Through our conversation, I learned that management at this specific location had been reducing staff, while increasing the number of appointments. Not surprisingly, this was causing long wait times. On average, people were waiting an hour for their appointments. Some people handled the situation without a problem and others did not.

While she was taking my blood, she shared a story with me about a man who did not take kindly to the delay. After about twenty minutes of waiting for his appointment, he started appearing at the window and asking how much longer he had to wait. He did this about every five minutes. In between his visits to the window, he paced in the waiting room. Needless to say, he was making the other patients a bit nervous. The technician could tell patients were nervous by the way they were peering over the tops of their newspapers or magazines, watching him.

As it approached almost an hour past his scheduled appointment, the man started to raise his voice a bit more. The technician said they were doing their best to keep up with the appointments. But he didn't like the answer and began to yell more. She tried to patiently talk to him and never said anything to offend him. He was already offended by the wait time, though, and he was prepared to take it out on her.

The man's behavior escalated and he then started to use profanity in his conversation. The technician asked him to be quiet; especially since there were children in the waiting area. He was not happy about that and yelled even more. At this point, the technician realized she needed to get out of the moment and couldn't do it alone. She proceeded to pick up the phone and call the police.

The man thought she was bluffing and continued on his rant. Since there was a patrolman nearby, the patient found out within two minutes the worker was not bluffing. The policeman escorted him out, and that was the last the office has seen of this patient. The technician understood his frustrations, after all she was frustrated with her own management. But she couldn't let this man continue to disrupt the office, so she called in the troops when she needed and ended the negative moment for everyone there.

❀ ❀ ❀ ❀ ❀ ❀

We are not suggesting that the police be called in every negative situation, but there is a time and a place for relying on others to help you get out of such a moment. We all need help sometimes. In the next story, Kris coaches her six-year-old son to find an adult when he needs help in a negative situation.

The Bully

By Kris

Our family belongs to a local YMCA chapter. Many times, while Gary and I work out, the kids are supervised by YMCA staff in areas designed for children of their own age group. Our son, Matthew has fun in a place called the Adventure Room. It's a space about as large as a gymnasium, with lots of adventure type activities— climbing, slides, ropes, etc. He enjoys going and playing with all the kids in such a unique environment.

One day, when I picked him up, Matthew seemed reserved and not particularly energetic. Normally when I pick him up, he's sweaty and practically bouncing off the walls from all of the activity. It took a while, but he finally told me that he did not have any fun that day. When I asked him why, he said it was because he just sat around by the door. My first instinct was he didn't feel good, however, that wasn't the problem.

The problem was a boy named Mark, who was in the Adventure Room that day. Supposedly, none of the kids liked him because he ran around and hit other kids with mats. He blocked kids from going down the slides and tripped them when they were running up the large hill in the Adventure Room.

I asked Matthew what the other kids did when this

happened. He said some kids hit him back, pushed him, or yelled at him. I asked Matthew how he reacted to Mark. He said he tried to stay away from him, but he got tired of running away all the time, so he went and sat by the door.

"Mommy, it was the only way I could get away from his meanness," Matthew added.

Matthew was faced with a negative situation, and he decided just to walk away and stay away. He removed himself from the moment by sitting near the door into the Adventure Room, where the teenage supervisors watch over the room. When I asked Matthew why the teachers didn't say anything about Mark's behavior, he said he didn't think they knew about it. According to Matthew, Mark was mean in places where the teachers couldn't see, like near the slides or behind the poles.

I told Matthew I thought he did well by just walking away from Mark. We discussed how being mean to someone because they are mean to you usually will not solve anything. In Matthew's words, "All that does, Mommy, is make you mean, too. That isn't nice."

I just love a six-year-old's 'spective. He summed it up so succinctly.

We continued our conversation about bullying and how it can make people feel. I asked Matthew if there was anything else he could have done while Mark was being mean to him. After a little prompting, and reminding Matthew of previous conversations we've had, he concluded he could ask an adult for help. In other words, he could rely on another person to get him out of the negative moment.

A week later, we were getting ready to leave for the Y and Matthew didn't want to go. When I asked him why, his answer was, "What if Mark is there?"

"That is a terrific question," I replied. "What if Mark

is there? What are you going to do?"

He said he would walk away and tell a teacher. I was hoping he had learned a life lesson from all of this.

As I walked up to the Adventure Room after my workout that day, I felt a little uneasy. I was hoping Matthew would not be sitting right next to the door waiting for me. Instead, what I saw was a pleasant surprise. There was Mark in the Adventure Room, playing with Matthew and three other boys. They looked to be having a terrific time. All of them were laughing, smiling, and running around.

When Matthew came out to meet me, I asked him what happened. He told me that Mark was picking on the kids, so Matthew walked away and told a teacher. The teacher had Mark sit down for a few minutes. When Mark came back to play with the kids, he was nice, and they all had a great time. Matthew was bubbly and excited to tell me about all his adventures that afternoon. This was a fantastic learning opportunity for him, and I presume it was probably a learning experience for Mark, as well.

❀ ❀ ❀ ❀ ❀ ❀

In Matthew's case, he relied on the teachers to help stop the negative moment for him and the other children. He had to learn how and when to ask for help, but when he did, the results were positive for all of those involved. Do you have someone you can count on to pull you out of a negative moment? In the next story, Kris relied on her husband to help end a negative and extremely messy moment for her.

Heavy Cream Explosion

By Kris

I was cleaning out our refrigerator after the Christmas holiday season and I found a half used container of heavy cream. It was a month past the expiration date printed on the pint size cardboard container. Most people would have just tossed it in the garbage. Yet I decided to empty the container before throwing it out. When I flipped it upside down, nothing came out. The cream on top had thickened, trapping the remaining cream underneath.

So I righted the container, and for some reason I decided the best approach would be to squeeze the sides of the carton. I thought it would loosen up the hardened cream. Then I would be able to dump it out in the drain, flatten the cardboard container, and throw it in the garbage.

That's not even close to what happened next. As soon as I squeezed the sides of the container, the liquid that was underneath the thickened cream sprayed directly out of the container with a force I would never have imagined. Of course, I was looking directly at the container as this happened.

The liquid and hardened cream went all over me. I had cream on my face, in my hair, and on all my clothes.

It was running down my neck and my sweater. The cabinets were coated, and the kitchen island was covered. It looked like a gallon of cream had been dumped all over the kitchen! I stood there in complete shock at what happened. In that one moment, I wanted to cry, laugh, and swear. I was so frustrated with myself. But the anger was beating out all the other emotions. I did not want to go to an angry spot, but it was quickly overtaking my thoughts.

How could I be so stupid?

What was I thinking?

What a mess!

This is going to be so hard to clean up!

I knew I was not pulling myself out of the negative spiral, so I yelled for Gary. He yelled back, "Are you okay?"

"Physically, yes," I answered. "But not on any other level."

When he walked in the kitchen, his expression was priceless. He had no idea what had happened to me. The engineer in him was trying to figure out what was all over me and the kitchen. It looked as though I had dumped a gallon of milk on my head and on the counter. I think he also wanted to laugh, but probably deduced by looking at the situation that it was not a good idea. He simply handed me a towel so I could stop the dripping, and all he said to me was, "Go get cleaned up."

I went upstairs and showered. By the time I got back to the kitchen, it, too was all cleaned up. I explained to Gary exactly what happened, and we had a good laugh over it.

❀ ❀ ❀ ❀ ❀ ❀

Gary took Kris out of the moment by first removing her from the situation. Then he stopped the moment from further affecting her by cleaning up the whole mess. It feels good when you have support like that.

Look for similar situations in your life when you can be of support. Maybe you can help someone get out of a negative moment and flip his or her tables! You may also start to recognize who helps you the most. Those types of people probably make you feel happier to be around them than those who try to create negative moments for you.

It is easier to get someone else out of a negative moment when you are feeling unaffected by the negativity yourself. You'll have more energy and more strength to focus on the other person. However, what do you do if the moment is negative for both of you, but for two different reasons? In the following story, even though Kris was running seriously low on positive energy, she recognized that her positive energy tank was fuller than her husband's. A hug is all it took to get him out of the moment and give Kris a little boost not to lose her cool.

Meatball Frenzy

By Kris

My family and I were at my in-laws' house, about an hour from home, for a long ski weekend. On the first morning, we awoke to find my daughter Sara sick. She appeared to have an ear infection. I am no doctor, but when there is yellow pus draining from an ear, it seems to be a pretty good indicator.

I drove Sara to our pediatrician in Buffalo while Gary and my son Matthew stayed behind to ski. I wanted to be with Sara, and I would never have traded places with Gary, but I still felt a bit sad about the situation. I had truly been looking forward to a day on the slopes with Gary and Matthew. My mother-in-law had planned to watch Sara while we skied. It was supposed to have been a pleasant, relaxing, outdoorsy day!

The round trip to take care of Sara, which included the doctor's office, pharmacy, lunch, and a stop at home for a nap (for her, not me) took about eight hours. I arrived at my in-laws' around dinner time. I had talked to Gary on the way back, and we finalized dinner plans— Swedish meatballs and noodles, a pretty easy dinner to pull together. I walked in the house and found the water for the noodles boiling over on the stove and the meatball sauce splattering everywhere. No husband was in sight.

It turned out he was actually upstairs making beds and putting away laundry.

When I called out to Gary, he came running down the stairs saying, "I knew I should have checked the food. I can't believe I forgot about it. What was I thinking?" He continued with expressions like this for a good two to three minutes. He even used the "s" word in front of Matthew, who was five at the time. Of course, this caused Matthew to go running around the house saying, "Daddy said the "s" word. Daddy said the "s" word."

Now bear in mind, the "s" word is not what you are thinking. The word is "stupid." Gary was calling himself stupid. All this frenzy was going on at a time when my energy level was essentially on empty. I had a long day of driving, doctor appointments, and a pharmacy visit with a two-year-old who had an ear infection.

At this particular moment, the easiest thing to do would have been to jump on the pity band wagon and complain to my husband that I couldn't believe he burned dinner and ask him what would we do. It was dinnertime and both kids were hungry, and so was I. I was tired and just wanted to have a relaxing night. But instead of verbalizing any of those words, I took a very deep breath and tried to find some positive energy from deep inside myself. It took me a minute, but I was actually surprised at the words that came out of my mouth.

"Honey, it's okay, we can order a pizza. It's just a pan of meatballs. It's really no big deal."

On the outside, it sounded good, but with every word I spoke, my thoughts were, *You've got to be kidding me. This was a simple dinner to make, meatballs and sauce. Really?* But then, surprisingly, more nice words came out of my mouth.

"Honey, just relax. You're winding the kids up. It's

all going to be okay. In the grand scheme of things, this really doesn't matter."

Picture the five-year-old, still running around about the "s" word. The two-year-old has no idea as to what's going on, but jumps into the mix. She must have been thinking, *Looks like a great opportunity to start running around and screaming*. It's surprising how kids sense the energy immediately.

While the kids were running around, Gary was trying to regain control over the meal. This was actually more difficult than you would think. He was cooking on a glass stove top. The week prior, someone cleaned the stove top and it was sparkling clean. But there was one problem: The cleaner had taken all the markings off the knobs. So there was no way to tell if the burners were on high, low, or off. In a moment of calmness, you would be able to take a deep breath and turn everything off. Then you would turn the knobs to about where you estimated you needed them.

Gary was doing anything but thinking straight. He was just randomly turning the knobs. When he would turn them in the wrong direction (higher), sauce would spatter even more. At this point, I began to recognize the humor in the situation and started to laugh. That didn't help Gary, but the kids loved it. They laughed harder and yelled, "Daddy said the "s" word" louder. Thank goodness the in-laws had gone out to dinner and were not part of this craziness.

I realized all my husband needed was a hug to calm him down. I got him to step away from the stove, gave him a loving hug, and said, "Let me take care of this."

Surprisingly, the hug instantly filled my positivity tank. I felt better, and that feeling of stress just floated away. It took a few minutes, but eventually Gary regrouped and told me he was just extremely disappointed. His plan was to have the laundry done (my son had an accident the night before, so we had to change the bedding) and have dinner ready for me when I got home. He knew I had a long day dealing with ear goop. He said he also figured that I was probably feeling sad for missing time with him and my son on the slopes. After hearing that, I sure was glad I hadn't jumped on the pity wagon with him in the kitchen! That would have broken my heart to have yelled at him, knowing he was only trying to do something nice for me.

We salvaged the meatballs and sauce that were at the top of the pan. The bottom of the pan was pretty black! We ate the meatballs with sauce, and the kids had plain noodles. We also all ate a lot of the fresh loaf of bread I had bought. The good news was that we all had room in our bellies for dessert. For some reason, that night the ice cream tasted better than it normally did.

❀ ❀ ❀ ❀ ❀ ❀

If Kris had yelled during the meatball frenzy, how would Gary have reacted? Maybe he would have yelled back. Maybe he would have walked away. In either case, he probably would have gotten more upset. By choosing to stay positive and trying to get him out of his moment, Kris shifted the outcome of that night. All Gary needed to help ease him out of his negative vortex was a hug. A simple hug was it. Sometimes nipping it in the butt is that simple.

And sometimes physically removing yourself from the situation may be your best option. In the next story, Kris describes a scenario where Gary just had to walk away from "it" to get out of his negative moment.

The Tractor Takes a Bite out of the Patio

By Kris

My husband Gary loves sales and deals. He enjoys going to auctions to try and find a "bargain." I'm not exaggerating when I tell you that he has come home with trailers full of stuff from auctions. Following the most recent one, he came home with two trailers and a truckload of wood for under $100. What a bargain!

When you buy all of this stuff, though, the problem is that you always have to find a place to put it. So we're always moving things around. Luckily, we have a tractor with a front loader to do all of the heavy lifting for us.

On this particular night, Gary was planning to deal with the 500-pound safe he bought at a scratch and dent sale. The sale was so great that he actually came home with two 500-pound safes. Thankfully he sold one, so we had just one left to bring inside.

Gary decided to use the tractor to first put the safe on our patio. Then he would drive the tractor up on our patio and gently put it in the house through our sliding glass door. Once it was in the house, we would figure out how to move it and where to put it.

Our patio is concrete and has two sets of stairs with

two steps each. When we began this endeavor, we assumed both sets of stairs were the same height. (Note to self: next time, verify this.)

With the tractor on the ground, Gary used it to lift the safe, and the pallet under it, onto the patio. He drove the tractor itself up the wide stairs and onto the patio. From there he used the tractor to pick up the safe and pallet again and gently place everything through our open sliding doors and into the house. We had one close call when the tractor's bucket almost hit the glass window, but no other issues.

Once the safe was in the house, we assumed the hard part was over. Yet if Gary wanted to go down the same stairs he drove up, he would have had to maneuver the tractor in a series of tight turns. The easier route was to back down the other set of stairs that was directly behind him. At the time, it seemed like a reasonable choice.

It turned out, the first step on this other set of stairs was two inches lower than on the stairs he drove up. We found this out as the tractor backed down. It loudly scraped the edge of the patio and took out a large chunk of it!

Eeeks! From the look on Gary's face, and the piece of concrete lying on the grass, I knew we were in a moment. The tractor was on the ground, Gary was safe, but you could tell he wanted to explode. He looked at the spot where a chunk of patio was missing, looked at me, and looked at the kids. I figured the kids were about to hear their first word of profanity ever in our presence. Surprisingly, Gary stepped off the tractor and just walked out of the yard without saying a word. We are fortunate to live next to a few acres of open woods, and he just headed toward the trees. He paced around for a little bit. I saw his hands go to his head a few times. And in a few minutes he returned. He actually looked calm.

I thought this was just the eye of the storm. I was wrong. He looked at me and said, "The tractor is okay, I'm okay, and I can fix the patio."

"Then, why did you walk away?" I asked. His response was as simple as, "I just needed to walk away from it."

Sometimes negative moments cause instant reactions, like in the patio story. Have you ever just told someone you needed a minute, and you then walked away to calm down? What about going for a run after an argument with someone? Removing yourself and taking time to compose your thoughts and considering your reaction to a situation usually will improve the moment for all those involved.

There are other times, though, when it may take you awhile to realize you are in a situation and you have to get out. Jeanie provides an example of multiple people choosing to get out of a negative situation because they could not flip the tables of what was happening around them.

The Dysfunctional Department

By Jeanie

There are people in this world who are not happy unless all those around them are miserable. They seem to thrive on stirring up trouble. I once worked with two men like that.

When I started my first real job, the team dynamics seemed to be fine. For the most part, everyone got along and enjoyed working together. I shared an office with two other employees and soon learned that one of them, Donald did his best to stir up trouble at every turn. It didn't affect the department too much until he became close friends with another coworker, Henry, who seemed to love negative energy. Together they created a cancer within the department that ate away at it until most of the people left.

As time went on, some in the department, through hard work, started to be recognized by management for their accomplishments. Donald and Henry didn't like the fact that others were being rewarded. Instead of working harder and introducing innovation into the department, they took the easier approach of putting other people down in order to raise their stature. They also worked to gather intelligence on the others in order to make themselves "valuable" to the boss by having inside information on everyone. And they used this information to undermine the others' efforts.

This duo also gossiped about everyone. They spread ugly rumors that were built by putting the worst spin on every situation. They even targeted a specific new employee. They didn't like her because her style was different from theirs. We were working for a small company and she had come from a large company. She was used to having more formal processes. They started equating her love of process to her wanting to "control" everything. They starting telling people she was a "control freak" and every time she made the slightest suggestion for improvement, it was characterized as another way she was trying to gain control. They painted her as a non-team player, and unfortunately, since she was a newcomer, coworkers believed Donald and Henry. Even though some of us tried to stick up for her and dispute the falsehoods, the damage had been done and other coworkers formed a negative perception of her. She was never able to fit in with her new team— Donald and Henry had completely undermined her credibility.

Eventually, Donald and Henry turned on just about everyone in the department. They made members of the work group distrustful of one another, and caused so much drama that everyone spent too much time obsessing about this situation. People were asking one another, "Did you hear what Donald and Henry said today?" There was so much negative energy caused by two people who insisted on presenting almost all situations in the worst possible light. A department that had good working relationships and team dynamics transitioned into a dysfunctional group with a complete lack of trust.

Some people stayed in the department, feeling they

could change the situation. Some people joined the duo and became negative along with them. It didn't make them feel good, but it did make them less of a target. Some people switched roles and moved to other departments. Others, like me, left the company completely. They just wanted to get away from the negativity, the constant drama, and worrying about their every move being scrutinized.

The idea here is that you can't always change a situation simply with positive energy or a different perspective. Sometimes you have to accept that a situation is toxic, and that you don't have the power to change it. It's at that point that you have to find a way to simply walk away. Negative people are insidious in their ability to sap our positive energy. Don't let them do it. You are in charge of your energy, and you must protect it.

❀ ❀ ❀ ❀ ❀ ❀

In the two previous stories, Jeanie and Gary removed themselves from a situation that was negatively affecting them. In Gary's story, he just needed time to cool down. In Jeanie's story, she needed to get out because it was affecting her well-being.

What happens if someone, say a child or animal, cannot remove themselves from a situation? Then it's up to you to make the hard decisions and take them out of the moment. In the next story, Kris provides an example of having to set aside her own emotions and fear and make a decision that gets a number of people out of a moment.

The Emergency Room Visit

By Kris

When my niece was six weeks old, one afternoon I received a phone call at work from my sister Kara. She sounded panicked and upset. My niece had been sick for a few days, and the doctor sent her for chest x-rays at a local hospital.

The technician read the x-rays immediately and told Kara it looked as if my niece had pneumonia. Those are some scary words to hear as you are holding a tiny, fragile six week old baby in your arms. He instructed Kara to take the baby immediately downstairs to the hospital's emergency room for admittance. My brother-in-law was out of town, so Kara asked me to meet her in the emergency room.

As soon as Kara arrived at the emergency room, she was informed they could not admit my niece as they did not have the proper facilities to handle infants. The staff told Kara that my niece would be transferred to a children's hospital about twenty minutes away. I offered to drive my niece and sister, but the hospital staff would not let us go since the baby was under their temporary care. They said the safest way to travel would be by ambulance.

An hour later, there was still no ambulance. There

had been some large traffic accident and all the local ambulances were assisting. We could have made it to the children's hospital and back in the time that we waited. My sister was stressing, and I could tell the nurses were getting nervous, too. They said my niece was dehydrated, and they wanted to give her an IV as we waited for an ambulance.

The nurses were sweet and kind, but since the hospital did not normally have infants in their emergency room, it was clear the nurses were not prepared for this. At least four nurses tried to insert the needle into my niece's arm. With every stick my niece screamed louder, and my sister cried more. My sister and I felt we were in the hands of professionals and should let them lead us. Yet after at least six attempts, I finally kicked the nurses out of the room. I lost my temper and told them, "Enough is enough. Get the ambulance and get us to the children's hospital, or I'll drive them myself."

Believe it or not, the nurses actually seemed relieved at my outburst. All they wanted to do was help my niece. I asked them to call the children's hospital and ask for advice. The pediatric doctors confirmed they needed a smaller needle for my niece, and this emergency room we were in was not equipped. The children's hospital doctor said my niece could wait for the IV as long as we could feed her with a bottle.

As soon as that call was finished, an ambulance arrived and my niece and sister boarded it. When they reached the children's hospital emergency room, the nurse had my niece hooked up and hydrating within seconds. And my niece actually slept through the entire process. Following a long night in the hospital, my niece was sent home and recovered fully.

There was nothing wrong with the nurses in the first

hospital. They just weren't faced with having to care for tiny babies as often as the children's hospital. Too often, we believe the medical profession knows better than we do, and we don't speak up. In this case, I had to take a stand for my niece and my sister. What I didn't expect was that the nurses would be just as relieved to have the moment stopped for them. When my sister and niece pulled away in the ambulance, the head nurse came over and chatted with me. She said she was extremely appreciative of what I did. In that moment, we all needed to take a step back and re-evaluate the situation. Removing my niece from the moment was exactly what we all needed.

It sounds so easy to say "get out of the moment" when you're involved in a negative situation. We all know when we're in the middle of one of those moments, sometimes we don't think very straight. You are ready to burst. You may want to yell at the top of your lungs, cry, or swear. Some people like to punch walls, kick things, or throw things. But that doesn't actually solve anything. Taking a moment to get out of "it" will probably calm you down faster than any of the more aggressive techniques. If you can calm your mind by leaving the moment, you will be able to deal with "it" more sanely.

Whatever it is that helps you get out of the moment, just do it as quickly as you can. Nothing good will come from staying in the negative moment any longer than you need to.

Chapter 8

Reflect on It

When the
It
Is Me

By the time you reach this chapter, hopefully you are recognizing your negative moments better than before you picked up this book. When you find yourself in negative situations, are you pausing and trying to look at the moment from a different angle? For the moments you cannot change, maybe you're able to find some peace to move forward in the moment, or maybe you've figured out how to get out of your negative moments.

What happens if you've tried all of that but the

moment still feels negative? Maybe you can't quite put a finger on it, but you know something is wrong and you can't see why. Could it be coming from you? Maybe *you* are "it." Maybe *you* are in a moment where a self-thought is dictating your outlook on a situation.

Often, self-thoughts start out as moment by moment type thoughts. Then they turn into patterns and habits whose origins are long forgotten. Negative self-thoughts can have a lasting negative effect on us and impact our lives in profound ways. These types of thought patterns can lower our self-confidence, lower our feeling of self-worth, and negatively impact our relationships, ultimately leading to a less desirable life.

A key to happiness is to take moments of negative self-thought and "nip them in the butt" quickly. This can stop any future negative thought patterns from settling in and becoming a habit. Once a habit is formed, we're dealing with "bigger than a moment" situations. We'll talk about those in one of our upcoming books in the Krispective series.

For the smaller moments, where self-thoughts are contributing to a negative situation, we'll share some personal stories that may help you understand what we're trying to communicate. We'll show you how we have dealt with these situations in our lives. It's not always easy, but with a positive attitude and a willingness to change, you can alter your own self-thoughts!

Have you ever set an expectation for yourself that you didn't meet? When you didn't achieve your plan, what types of thoughts were going through your head? Were they discouraging words that made you more upset, or were they encouraging thoughts that helped you move through the situation? Did you adapt and go with the flow, or did you continue to hold yourself to the original bar and perceive everything around you as failing? The next story shows you what happened when Jeanie set an expectation of hosting a flawless event.

The Reunion Disaster

By Jeanie

Years ago, when I lived in Western New York, I planned a family reunion to be held in Buffalo. My parents, brothers, sister, nieces, and nephews were all going to attend. A lot of us lived in different states and we hadn't been together in at least a year. We were going to have a cookout at my house, in my newly renovated backyard.

With the help of my friends and sister, I had recently built a stream and pond in my backyard, stocked with fish. Then, I had a new patio and awning installed. My backyard had been turned into a perfect vacation-at-home spot that I was so excited to share with my family. More importantly, I was excited to share a special day with special people in my life that I don't get to see very often.

I spent a lot of time preparing. I wanted the house to be perfect, the food perfect, the weather to be perfect, etc. You can already see the expectation I was setting for myself. There was no room for flaws. Of course, for the whole event to be perfect, I expected everything to be clean, too. I even decided I would make sure the grill was extra clean.

The night before the cookout, I brought the grill grate in the house, put it in the sink, and started cleaning it. Since it was not coming clean enough for me, I went to the store and bought some grill cleaner. That still wasn't really getting it clean, so I decided to use one of those oxygenated cleaners, hoping the oxygen action would power off the grime. Finally that worked, and the grate was sparkling clean. Perfect! Just as I planned it.

On the day of the picnic, I was ready. The house was clean, and the food and drinks were ready and on ice. We had sunny skies, but it wasn't too warm. Just perfect! My family started to arrive and we were all catching up and enjoying the tables full of snacks that were, of course, perfect. It felt so good to be in the presence of my family all in one place. I wish I could have captured the energy at that moment. Have I mentioned that it felt perfect?

The next series of moments, however, didn't quite meet my expectations, and they were far from perfect. It started out with, in hindsight, a very minor incident. As you learned in a previous chapter, my dog, Webster, is a large black Lab mix with a gentle, loving nature. He also is very curious, and his favorite activity is snacking. While we were all inside, he decided to check out the goodies on the picnic table outside. Luckily for me, all he could reach was the package of burger rolls. He had a tremendous feast and didn't show any signs of remorse that his gluttony could have ruined the meal (good thing there were extra hot dog rolls). I was not amused, but my family thought it was cute. There went my food being perfect!

The next not-so-perfect moment was when I noticed my kitchen drain was clogged. Nothing would go down it. My garbage disposal and the drain had been working the night before when I cleaned my grill and I had barely used the sink since then. It was going to be difficult to finish out the party without a functioning sink. So on the advice of my brothers, "It'll be quick, Jeanie. Just run to the store and buy some drain cleaner," I went to the store.

When I got home and poured in the drain cleaner, nothing happened. Luckily, I had bought multiple bottles, and I poured in another. At the time, it seemed like the most logical next step. In hindsight, no reaction with the first bottle should have been my clue that I had a bigger problem.

At this point, I had spent over an hour on the drain. This snafu was not in my plan. I was losing time to spend with my family, and I was getting more distraught. My brothers and brother-in-law jumped in and removed the pipe under the sink. Guess what? No sign of the blockage. This was definitely not perfect anymore, nor did it look promising that my perfect reunion was going to go very well.

I completely lost it and started crying. I wanted them to have a great time, and here we were dealing with this drain issue. My family all rallied around me. With a lot of hugs and words of encouragement, I started to feel better. They didn't view any of this as a big deal. It was just a clogged sink. We were all together. My brothers were actually having fun together trying to diagnose the problem. When you live states away from each other, you seldom get to bond often over household projects. As I simmered down, I noticed everyone was still laughing and having a great time. Maybe my perfect reunion was not ruined after all.

My brothers and brother-in-law didn't give up until we solved the clogged drain mystery. We finally diagnosed it as a ten-foot section of pipe in the basement that had to be removed and replaced. This meant a third trip to the hardware store in less than twenty-four hours. As it turned out, there was something unusual in the section of pipe we removed— a ten-foot long orange gelatinous mass that had been blocking the pipe. Our best guess was that it was a chemical reaction between all the stuff I had used to clean the grill and possibly the drain cleaner I used that day. Once we got the new section of pipe in, the drain worked fine. We ate dinner a little later than I had planned, and we had no hamburger rolls, but we still had a great time.

In hindsight, while all of the "negative moments" were happening, all I could think about was how I had ruined the perfect reunion. I was concerned about the impression I was making, and what my family was thinking about me. While I was worrying, I wasn't even noticing that despite all of the issues, everyone was having a great time. My self-thoughts took over and led me right down a negative path. I wasn't able to view the situation from any other angle until my family cheered me up and made me feel better. If I host a reunion again, I definitely won't set my expectations to have the perfect party. The party will be what it is, and that will be perfect just because the family is together, not because of how much planning or work I put into it.

In Jeanie's case, she realized partway through her day that although the reunion didn't meet her initial expectations, it was okay. She didn't need to worry about what everyone was thinking. No one was blaming her like she was blaming herself. Everyone actually had a good time.

Jeanie was able to turn her negative thought process around and enjoy the family reunion. Fortunately her family helped her "flip the tables" during the picnic and she was able to make the most of the remaining time she had with them.

How often do you hold yourself to unreasonably high

expectations? Does it add stress to your life? Could you reduce your own expectations? Maybe it will also reduce your stress level, and you may find yourself happier and smiling a lot more. It may also allow you more time to enjoy the important parts of life: like good friends and family.

In the next story, Kris will show you how her self-thoughts about a situation were so vastly different from a complete stranger's viewpoint. The story illustrates how quickly a moment can bring out insecurities in your self-thoughts. Good thing this stranger flipped her tables and nipped her negative self-thoughts right in the butt before she even realized what was happening.

The Skiing Split

By Kris

My husband has been an avid skier since he was two. My mother-in-law has a trail named after her at the resort where we ski throughout the winter. My father-in-law was a great skier who had taught many people how to ski throughout his fifty plus years of skiing.

When I met Gary, I had skied once in my life. Needless to say, as our relationship progressed, I knew skiing would become a big part of our lives. With such a great support system of strong skiers, I learned how to ski. I am nowhere as good as they are, but I can hold my own, most of the time anyway.

My daughter, Sara, was three years old the first winter we took her out skiing. She is a daredevil at heart and has a determination about her that is stronger than most adults I know. She enjoyed skiing from the minute we strapped the skis on her for the first time. However, with a three-year-old, you have to be careful as they don't understand the art of turning on the hill yet. They prefer to point their skis downhill and let them rip. They also aren't great with their directions. So if you say, "Turn left," there's a fifty percent chance they'll go left and a fifty percent chance they'll run right into the object you want them to turn away from.

To compensate for all that, Gary and I made a decision to teach both kids how to ski on a tether rope. The child wears a vest with a rope attached to it. While, the adult skis behind the child and helps control their speed, the child has full control to turn and learn proper skiing techniques. The tether provides a bit more safety for the child on the hill.

Skiing with a child on a tether requires quite a bit of leg strength, as you are using your quadriceps muscles most of the time to maintain a constant speed for the skiing child. Gary is a much stronger skier than I am, so he normally would ski with Sara. When she fell down, he magically stopped on a dime and picked her up, and both of them would be skiing again within seconds. He made the whole process look so easy, when in reality he was just showing off what a terrific skier he was. When he would ski behind her on the tether for hours, he never complained about how tired he was, and his patience never faltered. It is his teaching style that contributed to both of our children loving to ski.

Then, there was my style of skiing with Sara. I am a pretty good skier, but nowhere near an expert like Gary. When I skied on the tether with Sara, I was exhausted halfway down the hill. My legs would be so sore, I would have to make her stop so I could rest. When Sara would fall, it took me a lot longer to get in position, pick her up, and straighten her out on the hill. I know for a fact we did not look as seamless as when Gary scooped her up after a fall. Probably at least one out of every four times she fell with me, I ended up falling just trying to pick her up. If you aren't a skier, you're probably thinking, "*What's the big deal. Just pick up the three-year-old and move on. What can be so hard about that?*"

Remember, most of the time she had fallen because

of ice, or maybe we were on a steep section of the hill. So when I would have to pick her up, that meant I was on ice or a steep part of the hill with two wooden sticks strapped to my feet, trying to reach out and pick up a thirty-pound limp child.

Despite my feeling of inadequacy in tether skiing, I would continue to give it a shot each week. I was trying to nip my negative self-thoughts. I thought if I just kept trying, I would get better at it. I would try and focus on the quality time I was having with Sara and not how hard it was for me to pick her up when she fell. There is something magical about being on a ski hill in the fresh air with your three-year-old, so I kept trying to concentrate on those thoughts.

On one particular day it was forecasted to be 20 degrees Fahrenheit, so I put on a heavier than normal wool sweater. About ten minutes into that morning, I realized I was overdressed. I was very warm, but we weren't near the lodge for me to drop off my sweater. When I get too hot skiing, I can get a bit cranky, or at the very least my positive attitude is not in the game. Yet I was determined to keep working on my tether skills, overdressed or not.

It was a beautiful, bright morning with fresh powder. Gary truly enjoys having some of the first tracks down the hill, so I encouraged him to leave Sara and me and go enjoy the mountain with Matthew. As soon as he left, Sara started to act a little whiny. Normally she starts every morning skiing with Gary, so I thought the change in plans threw her off a bit. Three-year-olds like structure and schedule. She didn't seem to try as hard as she normally does when she skies down the hill with Gary. She fell more than normal which meant I spent a lot of time trying to get her back up and skiing again.

I tried being as patient and positive as Gary was

when he skied with her.

"C'mon, you are doing great!"

" Let's sing songs as we ski down."

"Let's pretend we're an airplane as we ski left to right."

"What a great turn that was!"

"It's okay that you fell. Let's get up and keep going."

This went on for over an hour. It was so hard to keep up the encouragement, as I was heating up with every fall. I have never enjoyed chairlift rides as much as that day. It gave me a moment to breathe and cool down. Since we were on the beginner hill, the chairlift ride was very short. And every time we got back up to the top, my positive attitude faded some.

At one point Sara told me it wasn't as much fun skiing with me as with Daddy. Ugh. There went another chink in my positive attitude. On another one of her falls, she told me that Daddy knew more than me about picking her up." Ugh, again. There wasn't much positive juice flowing through me anymore, I was drained dry.

Then, when we got down to the bottom of the hill, she told me she couldn't continue. Sara was too tired. We were about one hundred feet from the lift line. Somehow, I smiled, and I told her it was alright. I planned to just push her by skiing, or in my case "waddling," behind, with her in between my legs.

For those of you who ski, you know it takes a lot of work to walk on skis with a child between your legs. I was giving it all the energy I had left when she decided to just throw herself down spread eagle, bottom up in the air. As she did that, she pushed my skis out away from each other and down I went, spread eagle, too. In hindsight, I have no idea how my legs stretched as far as they did. There I was, bent over Sara with my legs stretched farther out than ever in my whole life, and she was under me in the exact same position. All I wanted to do was fall to the ground, but I couldn't. I was stuck, bottom in the air and not going anywhere. As I'm writing this, I am actually laughing out loud. I can only imagine what it looked like. I was literally stuck in this position and had no idea how I could get out of it. At that moment, I just wanted to cry.

Then, this kind, sweet lift attendant came over and pushed my left ski towards my right ski very slowly and gently. It was just enough to provide my body with an angle to get up. She even bent down and picked Sara up for me.

I was so frustrated with myself, so upset at my ability to ski, and all I wanted to do was either yell at Sara or cry. It was at that moment that the lift attendant looked at me and asked, "How old is she?"

I told her three. "You are so brave for bringing her out," she replied. "It's really hard to ski with them sometimes when they are that young. They have a hard time focusing. But don't worry, it will be worth it. Starting them out young creates a love for the sport that lasts a lifetime."

I knew she was right. I was so focused on how I was not as good as Gary at handling Sara, I never thought about how many people wouldn't even be able to do what I was doing. I was a better skier than I was giving myself credit for. That lift attendant stopped my negative self-thoughts instantly and I enjoyed the rest of my day thoroughly (even though my legs were a bit sore from my almost split).

❀ ❀ ❀ ❀ ❀ ❀

In this skiing story, Kris recognized her negative self-thoughts and was able to combat them with the help of a complete stranger. What happens when people don't even realize they have negative self-thoughts? Negative thoughts can lead to negative outcomes. If it's true that you become what you eat, then do you also become what you think? See what you think after you read the next story.

Go and Win Baskets!

By Kris

On this particular Thursday, my employer had sponsored a basket raffle to benefit the American Cancer Society. Multiple individuals and departments had donated baskets of all kinds for the event. There was even a kayak in the auction. For a 200-person company, this event raises a lot of money and draws nearly everyone out of their cubicles to participate. Some even say it the biggest supported and most attended employee event of the year.

As with traditional basket raffles, you buy tickets and place them into the bags for whichever prizes you want to win. I personally love basket raffles. Whenever I have a chance, I go to them. It's a joke with my dad and my husband. Anytime we see a sign advertising a basket raffle, they always point it out to me and ask if we're changing plans to head to the event.

I like donating to the charities, but I also love the anticipation of the coordinator announcing the numbers and waiting to hear my number called. Gary and I have a reputation for wining at basket auctions. One year, when we were both working at the same company, they announced our name so many times, I was embarrassed. I am still teased about that auction at work. Gary actually had to go home and get a trailer to haul all of our winnings, which included four work benches!

Recently, we went to a family event at Matthew's school. There were ten baskets for about 300 people. We won two of the baskets. We only bought $20 worth of tickets. Another time Gary and I went to a basket auction with my father at a fire hall. Again, we each spent $20. Between the three of us, we won so many times we didn't think everything would fit in the car!

Some people just call us lucky. However, I realized on this particular Thursday at the American Cancer Basket Auction, that my winning may be part luck but it's also part attitude. As I was putting my tickets in the bags, I listened to the talk around me.

"I told my husband today I was just donating to the charity. I don't know why I bother putting in the tickets."

"I am not lucky."

"I never win."

"My odds of getting hit by lightning are better than winning a basket."

This type of talk went on and on while I put my tickets in bags for the baskets. As the comments continued, they were making me laugh. Yet, with every ticket I put in, I just thought about what I would do with the prize when I won it. Notice I used the word "when," not "if." Using the word when "puts it out there" that I will win. No negative thoughts about losing crossed my mind, only positive thoughts about winning. At that point, it truly was all happening subconsciously in my mind. I hadn't really tuned into the negativity, probably because everyone was laughing and joking about it. I was doing my own thing and being positive Kris.

Later in the day, it was time for the tickets to be drawn. I went downstairs very uplifted and excited. I was on my way to winning at least one basket, maybe two, but not more because I didn't want to be embarrassed. If people are still picking on me about an auction from over seven years ago, I'm sure it would only get worse if I were to win three or more baskets again. So I decided it would be one or two baskets, and I would be happy with anything I won.

I sat down with a group of ten people or so, and the negativity resumed. Of course, whenever people made their statements, they were smiling or laughing just like when we were putting our tickets in the bags. However, this was a completely different set of folks than those who were around me when I entered the tickets. It was then that I started to think about the amount of negativity coming from each person despite, the laughing and smiling. It was a joke to them, but they were actually creating their outcomes.

"They'll never draw my numbers. I don't win anything."

"I'm a loser. No chance here."

"I come close to winning numbers, but it's never mine they call out."

"In ten years of these auctions, I have never won."

That last statement caused me to respond. I looked up and said, matter-of-factly, "I win every year."

And no joke, as soon as I said that, the basket coordinator read my number. I won a kids' gardening basket. Everyone at the table was shocked. In all honesty, I wasn't surprised at all. I win baskets.

"How did you just do that?" asked the man who had never won a basket.

"Simple," was my answer. "It's all in the attitude. I just believe I'll win and then I do."

Guess what he said next? "Well, I guess I believe I'll lose and then I do. We balance each other."

Ugh! I thought. How icky to surround yourself with that attitude. If he was creating that energy for himself at a basket raffle, I could only imagine what he was doing in more important situations, like with family or customers. I try very hard to never judge a person, but I do find it difficult to understand why someone would choose that negative path.

As I reflected on all of the negative comments I heard at the auction, I realized these were all negative self-thoughts. Each person was down on themselves because they never won. Their negative thoughts were actually creating a negative outcome for them. It really is amazing how your own words can create the energy around you. What feels better to you?

"I am a loser" or "I am going to win a basket."

"I never win a basket" or "I always win baskets."

Simple word changes really can impact your life in a big way. Start small and easy. It is a process, but if you work at it, you will feel the change in your attitude about every moment.

I'm not saying that I won just because of my attitude.

I think luck does have something to do with it. But I go in positive, and on the off chance I do lose, I'm not mopey about it or negative. I always think to myself, *I will get one at the next raffle.* So go out there and win lots of baskets! What do you have to lose?

In the previous stories, we showed how you can nip negative self-thoughts in the butt when you stop, recognize them, and adjust your attitude. Maybe it is simply changing the words you use, or looking at the situation from a different angle. Wouldn't it be nice if those negative thoughts never even crossed your mind? The following story illustrates how children can be in the same situation as an adult, but all they see is the positive side. Negative thoughts do not even enter a child's mind sometimes.

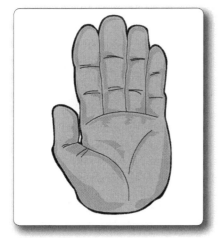

I Have a Left-Hand

By Kris

It was May of 2012. Summer had come early to Buffalo, New York that year, as it did throughout the East Coast. On this particular day, my family and I had a great summer day. An early morning walk, hot dogs on the patio for lunch, an afternoon of creek walking, followed by some ribs on the grill for dinner. And all of that topped off with ice cream at our favorite farmers market for dessert. It sure doesn't get much better than that!

After our ice cream run, I took Sara upstairs for a bath and Gary took Matthew outside for a bonfire. As I was watching Sara play and giggle in the bathtub, I was happy, and feeling like 2012 might be turning around for me. The year had started out rough. In January, there was a reduction in the staff at the company where I worked and I had to say goodbye to many of my friends. In February, my mother caught pneumonia and died of a secondary infection within three weeks. Then, in March, Gary had an accident and found himself in the emergency room, getting more than twenty-five stitches on his knee. He was on crutches for a while, but overall, he was fine.

It had been a stressful few months, yet here I was watching my daughter in the bathtub, feeling like one of the "luckiest girls in the planet." (Yes, another Krisism. It's on Jeanie's list). I smiled as Sara sudsed up all her mermaids. At that moment, things seemed to be settling down. I was truly thankful for all the goodness in my life. I knew that even though I had faced losses that year, I didn't have to look far to see blessings.

Watching Sara in the bathtub reminded me of how carefree children are. She was truly enjoying one of life's pleasures, a warm bath with lots of bubbles. Kids really do enjoy the moment. No negative thoughts were impeding her at all. How perfect!

After her bath, we snuggled and read books and had a very peaceful bedtime. It feels so good when you put your child to bed like that. As you are tucking them in, you can just sense the peace, and you know they will get a good night's sleep. As I closed her door, after tucking her in, I was relaxed and looking forward to sleeping peacefully, too. However, I was quickly jolted into a completely different feeling.

Gone was the peaceful, happy, and carefree energy. I was in a moment where all I could hear was my son screaming downstairs. Only a mom can differentiate between a child's cries. There are a lot of them: the "I am tired" cry, the "I am hungry" cry, the "I am faking it to get attention" cry, the "I am hurt but not too badly" cry, and then there is THIS cry. It was a cry I had never heard, but I knew. I knew something was terribly wrong.

I flew down the stairs so fast I don't even remember my feet touching them. I found my husband and Matthew in the bathroom. Gary was holding Matthew's hands under cold water and Matthew was begging him to stop. Gary looked scared. And Gary never looks scared. He is calm in every situation. This is the man who bandaged his own knee after he cut it with a chainsaw. So I knew it must be bad if Gary was scared.

I could see that Matthew's hands were bright red. Gary then told me Matthew slipped and was falling into the bonfire coals when he braced himself for the fall with his hand, specifically, his right hand. Honest to goodness, my first words were "Thank God, it wasn't his face." In that moment of shear panic, I was thankful for something. Yes, I was terribly scared for Matthew and I wished with every part of my being I could take the pain away, yet I was so thankful he didn't go face first into the hot coals. That instant of gratitude gave me strength to deal with the negative moment. That is how I found peace.

I took some deep breaths and leaned down to talk to Matthew. I thought maybe I could distract him. He was still screaming and begging me to make Daddy stop. It broke my heart, but I had to be strong. I didn't want him to see me cry or appear afraid. I held his left hand and just kept telling him it would be alright. Between every sentence I took deep breaths. Similar to taking a breath to help stop negativity in its tracks, I was taking breaths to stay calm in the moment.

After consulting with medical professionals, and understanding we were dealing with second-degree burns, we knew we didn't have to take him to the hospital. We wrapped Matthew's hand in ice-cold towels and gave him the recommended pain medicine. Eventually, he fell asleep on the couch. We took turns sleeping next to him all night just to make sure he was okay and to change the towels if needed.

I was afraid of what would happen when he woke up. I assumed he would be in a lot of pain and not able to do much. In hindsight, I can't believe I had those negative thoughts. Why didn't I think positively and believe he would be okay in the morning? As you will see, it took the six-year-old to remind me to stay positive.

When Matthew woke up in the morning, his hand was full of blisters and looked worse than I ever imagined it would. What surprised me the most though was Matthew's attitude. I was prepared to keep him home from school for a while to tend to his wounds and let him heal. After all, he was right-handed and this was a pretty severe injury to his right hand. Matthew's response was simple: "Why would I have to stay home, Mommy? My left hand still works! Let's just bandage my right hand."

This was the worst accident of his life and he didn't even see it as something to slow him down. In his mind, it was just a nuisance and he had a perfectly good hand to keep using. I wonder, if that were me, how many days of work would I have missed? I bet more than one. But to this young boy, it was no big deal. The pain was gone, so he was ready to move on with his life.

We talked to the nurse at school and determined he could attend classes, as long as he stayed out of some gym activities. He had a bandage on his hand for about two weeks. We had to make sure no dirt got in any of the sores once the blisters popped. Throughout that time, Matthew never complained, except to tell us we were bothering him too much by asking him how he felt.

"I told you, it's fine," he would say with an exasperated voice.

About a month after his hand was healed, we ran into the school nurse after a school program, and she commented on how well Matthew handled the whole situation. I believe it was due to his attitude, he saw no reason to be negative. It's too early to tell if Matthew's positive attitude will last him for a lifetime, but I sure hope he carries this with him as a lesson!

Reflecting back, I was able to stay calm in the

moment, however, I struggled with being overly optimistic about the situation. While I was lying in the recliner with Matthew sobbing on me, I could not have imagined in my wildest dreams that within twelve hours he would be in school, acting as if nothing ever happened. Matthew showed me how to just take life moment by moment and see where I am! Next time I'm faced with a situation like this, I think I'll ask myself, "Well, do I still have my left-hand?"

❀ ❀ ❀ ❀ ❀ ❀

How do we start to work on changing our negative thoughts so they don't even cross our minds? After all, we aren't like young Matthew, where negative thoughts haven't been impressed on him throughout his life. He doesn't even know how to think negatively. He is optimistic and positive. And what other way is there to be?

In the left hand story, Kris touched on a powerful tool to help negative self-thoughts. It's simply having a feeling of gratitude, or being thankful for something. When you recognize the good in your life, the "bad" doesn't seem so bad anymore.

One tool we have used is a gratitude journal. This is where you write down the things that make you feel thankful. You can do it as often as you want, but daily seems to work best for us when we're in a slump and need some constant positive thought reminding.

In the next story, the names have been changed to protect the innocent, but the foundation of the story is as close to factual as possible.

Martha Turns It Around

By Kris

Martha never had a nice thing to say about anything. In her mind, nothing good happened to her, and she sure as heck never won anything. She was definitely like one of the people at the basket raffle who participated just to donate to the charity. She had no expectations of actually winning.

She wondered to herself a lot as to why she didn't have many friends and why she seemed mopey all the time. She was often tired, and a big night out for her was normally when she joined her coworkers at the company happy hours that everyone was invited to. But even when she attended, no one really wanted to spend much time with her.

Martha felt like she was alone in the world, and was uncertain as to the reason. She was a hard worker and a caring person. She remembered people's birthdays and anniversaries and really did try to help others when she could. Somehow, though, she didn't seem to have any close friends or lasting relationships.

Yet, after reading one of those self-help books that suggested creating a gratitude journal, Martha sat down one night and got started.

Day #1 (Friday). Today I went to the bookstore and bought this journal. Seems like a dumb idea to write down what I am thankful for, but I am going to try it. That overpriced book and crazy author thought it was a good idea to focus on the things you have rather than the things you don't have. What does that author know anyway? I bet she is famous and rich. She couldn't possibly know what I need. She is probably in cahoots with the journal manufacturers. I am sure those guys are rich, too. These are exactly the type of things that sell great at the holidays.

Okay, anyways, back to the point. What am I thankful for today? I guess I am thankful it is Friday.

Day #2 (Saturday). Yesterday's entry didn't help me at all. I don't think this is going to work. I just don't see the point. How can a few words on a piece of paper "change my life" as the author of that cheesy self-help book claims? One of my faults, though, is if I make a commitment to something, I will stick with it. So I committed to trying this for at least a week. Even if it is a waste of my time, I will go through with it. I am not a quitter. I still can't think of anything creative to be thankful for, so I will basically copy yesterday's entry.

I am thankful it is Saturday.

Day #3 (Sunday). I really don't think this thing is working. It is pretty silly. I spent $15 on this journal and I think I probably wasted my money. Seriously, why should I be thankful for anything? I work hard, I buy what I need, do what I want. I rely on myself. That is life. I can't say I am thankful for Sunday because I don't like Sundays. That means tomorrow is work. I really don't like my job. It pays the bills though, and I get benefits. I wish I was doing something related to my college education. That probably won't happen. The economy sucks right now.

I guess I can be thankful I have a job, even if I don't like it that much.

Day #4 (Monday). I talked to Laurie today. She got laid off from work this morning. She had no idea it was coming. She was completely blindsided and is very upset. I struggled to find words to comfort her. I am thankful I still have a job. Since I don't want to copy from yesterday's entry, I need to come up with something else. It wasn't a rule from that fancy rich author, but it doesn't seem right to use the same item more than once. I know I did that on Friday and Saturday, but if I am going to try this, I want to give it a fair shot now.

I am thankful I have enough money to pay my bills, save a little, and have some spending money. Laurie is really worried. I am glad that isn't me. Wow. That is two new things I am thankful for.

Day #5 (Tuesday): Work wasn't so bad today. I got to work with James a lot and he is pretty good with the customers. He taught me some new sales techniques that helped me. I found that I was smiling more at work today.

I am thankful I have a job where I have opportunities to learn.

Day #6 (Wednesday): I talked to Laurie today. She is very discouraged. So many companies require a four-year degree and she never finished college. She doesn't think she can find a job making the same money she was. She is wondering how she will afford her apartment. I am glad I don't have that worry now.

I am thankful I had an opportunity to go to college.

Day #7 (Thursday): Well, it has been 1 week. It is crazy, but I think this journaling thing may be helping a little. It made me look at some of the positives in my life. I also enjoy doing this right before bed. It almost forces me to go to sleep on a happy note.

Who would have thought? Me...happy? It is only at this moment, but that's okay, I will keep working on it.

I am thankful I can be happy for a moment. One moment at a time.

Once Martha started to realize she actually had something to be thankful for, finding other things to be grateful for became easier. This thought process can change your outlook on your moment, your hour, or your day. Eventually it can affect the outlook on your week, your month, your year, and your overall perspective on life. Appreciating your blessings can help nip negative self-thoughts in the butt."

It may not happen overnight, but with continual work and self-reflection, you can change your outlook on your moments and your life. However, even when you think you have the most positive attitude and can deal with any situation, negative self-thoughts can still creep in and may catch you totally off guard.

In the next story, Kris will share with you what happened to her at her first Krispective outing. In hindsight, it makes her laugh, but in that moment she was panicking and the negative self-thoughts were nipping her.

What Am I Doing?

By Kris

The Preface covered how Jeanie and I ended up writing this book. Neither of us have formal training in writing, advertising, or publishing. But, we tackled it anyway. Why? Because we wanted to. We thought we could make a difference in at least one person's life. It felt like the right thing to do. So we moved forward with our plan to write one book.

Jeanie and I are both overachievers, with type A personalities. As it normally happens with the two of us, what started out as something small with a definitive end turned into a large-scale project with no end in sight. One book quickly turned into two books, and then three books. Those ideas for three books ended up as part of a formal five-year plan that may involve us training or consulting one day, should our path take us. in that direction.

If we were going to tackle so much, we decided to start a company, launch a blog, buy some domain names, and the list goes on. It was all exciting and fun, and it felt like we were on an adventure together. I had nothing but positive thoughts and feelings about our future, until the very first time I ventured out as an employee of Krispective, Inc.

I signed up for an intellectual property seminar at

a local university. If we were starting a company that involved copyrighting, we thought it would be best if we understood more about the topic. I was so excited on the morning of the seminar. I have attended many seminars before, but all for my regular job. I enjoy learning, meeting new people, and sharing my thoughts with the teams I am sitting with. I am outgoing and sociable in these types of settings. At least, I normally am.

I walked into the seminar room and the greeter asked me for my name and company. Saying "Kris Fredricks" was a piece of cake. When I went to say "Krispective," I froze. I could not utter the word. It was if my brain stopped working and I forgot how to talk for a few seconds.

At first I thought it was only because I have been with my "real" job for twenty years and I am so accustomed to saying that company's name. But, it was more than that. My stomach was doing flips and I actually started sweating. I thought, *What is going on?* Finally, after what seemed like eons, I said, "Krispective," and the woman behind the table welcomed me kindly and handed me a name tag.

It was a simple tag: "Kristen Fredricks" on one line and "Krispective, Inc." on the next line. For some reason, panic started to creep into my body. There were so many thoughts racing through my mind.

I actually have to wear a name tag that says Krispective.

What if someone asks me what I do?

What if a person asks me about the company?

Who am I to tell anyone about positive attitudes?

I am just a regular person with no training in this field.

What gives me the right to co-author a book and actually create a company to do it?

Yes, all negative thoughts, but I could not stop them. I was having some major self-doubt. I was so nervous I didn't make eye contact with anyone, and I made a beeline for a table, holding my portfolio up so it would block my name tag. After I sat down, I whipped out my phone and immediately texted Jeanie. Instead of telling her I was losing it, I decided to try to be positive. Maybe it would turn me around and flip my tables.

> **Jeanie, I am here. Our company has officially sent their first person to a training class. Yeah!**

In that moment, I felt good, but as people started to fill in at my table, my fear grew and I was going crazy again.

The class wasn't starting for fifteen minutes, and I felt that if I stayed at the table someone would strike up idle chitchat and ask what I did. Normally, I love that part of a training class. Not this time. Instead, I went to the buffet table and ate standing up; I went to the bathroom— twice; and I even walked the halls of the training center, all to kill those fifteen minutes. I kept telling myself to get a grip, but the anxiety kept building.

Finally, the class started and the instructor explained the course. It would be sixty minutes of lecture and sixty minutes of case work with your team at the table. The negative, fearful thoughts visited me again:

Oh, crud. I'm actually going to have to talk to people. I am sure they'll want us to introduce ourselves. What am going to do?

As it turned out, the lecture part was great and the instructor was dynamic and very knowledgeable on the subject. He grabbed my attention immediately and I forgot all about the table work that was coming up. So when we did have to introduce ourselves I was almost relaxed again. There was a little bit of fear lingering, though, because I did consider for a moment what I would do if I said "Krispective" and the group broke out in laughter and questioned my company. As I'm sure you have guessed, no one laughed at me. It was all in my head. After I made my introduction, the person sitting next to me immediately introduced himself.

Working through the case studies was fun, but I was very self-conscious of my name tag. Anytime someone looked at it, I wondered what they were thinking. As soon as class was over, I bolted out of there. I got in my car and felt so relieved, yet upset at the same time.

What was wrong with me? I was so excited to start this company. What just happened?

I couldn't call Jeanie because she was at her full-time job. Luckily, Gary was driving four hours to a customer's site that day. I knew he would be on the road, so I called him and explained the situation.

Gary immediately started laughing. He said the thought of me walking around with a binder covering my name tag was just "cracking me up," to quote him exactly.

Then he became serious and said, "Honey, you just felt what it feels like to be the rest of us."

"What do you mean?" I asked.

"Most of us are not positive like you all the time. Most of us do have negative self-thoughts. Most of us do have fears about things and sometimes those fears drive some negative thoughts. Starting a company is a big deal. Writing a book and putting yourself out there is personal. All your family, friends and coworkers know you and Jeanie are doing this. You are taking a risk. You were just in a situation by yourself where this all became 'real.'"

He was absolutely right. I wish I had called him when I was walking all over trying to kill those first fifteen minutes before class. I was afraid. I was starting a potentially new career doing something I was not formally trained in. I was writing a book that I wasn't sure people would want to read, let alone pay for. What if we failed?

Then the "AHA" light bulb went off and my negative self-thoughts were instantly nipped. There is no way we could fail. Even if not a single person, other than those we knew, bought the book, we still wrote a book. That is a huge accomplishment. And to add icing to the cake (another 'ism), we had a blast doing it and grew closer as friends. That is a true blessing!

The fear was gone and the anxiety disappeared. I'm sure it will pop up once in a while in the future. Yet I believe that is totally normal. Hopefully, I will recognize when it does, focus on the positive, and continue to move forward.

❀ ❀ ❀ ❀ ❀ ❀

Sometimes fear can cause you to pause, slow down a bit, make you think about your situation, and allow you the time to make good decisions. At other times, though, fear can limit you and keep you from moving forward. If you feel afraid, stop and think about what is driving your fear. Take some deep breaths and focus on nipping it in the butt with positive thoughts.

Your own thoughts about the environment you are living or working in can have a direct impact on how you are feeling.

Look at your life from another angle and you may get a different perspective. We are not implying you can change your self-thought process overnight, but if you address it a moment at a time, you can often shift your thoughts to a more positive direction. And as you do, you may feel yourself smiling more and thinking happy thoughts. Trust us, it will get easier with every smile or every laugh. You just have to be willing to try. As you become happier with your self-thoughts, you may find the people around you become happier, too. Now that's definitely something to smile about!

Chapter 9

Wrap It Up

We appreciate you taking time away from your busy life to read our stories and listen to our outlook on staying positive, even when you're faced with challenges. Nipping negativity in the butt is truly a journey of discovery and rediscovery. When you continue to hone these techniques we have introduced, you will learn more about the people around you. But more importantly, you will learn about yourself and how you can give yourself the gift of a more positive life.

We have found that using these techniques gets easier with awareness and practice. In summary, we hope you will remember to:

❀ **Recognize it.**
Learn to recognize when you are in a negative situation. Remember Kris' crazy Christmas or Jeanie's doggone camping trip? Think about who you interact with, the situations around you, and how you can use your negative vibe indicators to recognize a negative moment.

❀ **Pause it.**
Stop, breathe, and assess the situation. Think about how Gary handled the ruptured hose or how Jeanie dealt with her car accident. Using a few seconds to pause and assess the situation can help you take the emotion out of the moment and change the direction of an otherwise negative circumstance.

❀ **Nip it.**
The following bullets have suggested actions for nipping negativity.

- **Spin it.**
  View it from a different angle. Try to find the positive in the negative moment. Remember how Kris used this technique on a snowy day in Buffalo and ended up having an enjoyable day with her kids? Remember how Jeanie's friend, Walter, found that with a different perspective, his view of his boss turned into a great learning experience? Practice looking at

people and situations differently so you can change your view of them.

- **Don't sweat it.**
  Assess whether it really matters in the grand scheme of life. What's the big deal with a pair of soggy underwear or a chewed up futon mattress? Remember, what seems important today might not even be a memory next week.

- **Accept it.**
  Accept that it is negative, you can't change it, and find peace in the moment. Whether, like Gary, you've lost your wallet, or like Jeanie, you've locked yourself out of your car on a cold winter's night, sometimes you just can't change negative moments and need to look for ways to accept them.

- **Leave it.**
  Walk away from negativity. Remember how Kris' son used this technique to deal with a bully, or how Kris used it to deal with spilt milk (or cream, in Kris' case)? There are simply times when you can't change a person or situation and just have to remove yourself.

- **Reflect on it.**
  See if you are causing negativity in your own life. Think about Jeanie's attitude about her family reunion or Kris' 'spective on her skiing ability. Those around us took the situations in stride, but our negativity came from within.

Practice looking inside to see if you are the negative factor in a situation.

We hope you have enjoyed our stories and that they have helped to reinforce the techniques we've described for minimizing negativity in your life. We have found that articulating those negative moments for this book has also made both of us more aware of negative situations involving us and others.

Our original goal was to write this book, help one person in some way, and leave a legacy for the next generation of Wades and Fredricks. Yet the positive energy generated from the writing process, along with discussing techniques to combat negative energy, fueled our imaginations every day. The fun we had working together propelled us forward each day. As we continued, it was like peeling the proverbial onion, with many layers of moments to explore. So many thoughts came to us, it was clear there were simply too many to include them all.

One of the ideas that could not be included in this book, but came to the forefront while working on it, was the idea of "flipping the tables" for complete strangers when they were facing a negative moment. Could it be done?

To delve into this concept further, we paid extra attention to strangers when we were out in public and we watched for negative moments. Examples included a stranger being treated negatively by a clerk, someone's child melting down in a restaurant, and another person dropping eggs on a grocery store floor.

We found the answer was a resounding "yes," we could flip the tables for a stranger! It was an interesting experiment and affected people in quite a positive way. We were actually amazed at the reactions we received. We decided our next project will capture all sorts of "flipping the tables" interchanges with people. We are well underway with that book, and every table flipping gives us even more energy to try with more strangers.

As you can probably tell, writing this book has been an exciting adventure for us. It's highlighted areas in our own lives where we could be more positive. Our final story comes from Jeanie, and it shows how, even though she has been applying these positivity techniques and principles for years, there is still room to learn about nipping negativity.

Stuck in Traffic

By Jeanie

I hate traffic. I always have. I am generally impatient and I would be happier if everyone would stay out of my way so I can get where I'm going. One day recently, I was making my way to work and I was running a bit late for an early meeting. It seemed like every slow person in Maryland was on the road and getting in my way. I was getting more and more frustrated, and then I remembered that Kris and I had a book meeting later that night. It was enough to snap me out of the moment.

Sitting there in traffic, I had a revelation. I had no control over the other drivers. They could not hear me yelling in my car for them to get out of my way. There was nothing that I could do from inside my car that would change what they were doing inside their cars. So me being worked up about it was only frustrating me. I asked myself, "Why am I making myself feel negative and grumpy about a situation I cannot change?"

I immediately accepted that I was not going to be able to influence the situation. Suddenly, I felt at peace. I put on some of my favorite music, took some deep breaths, and enjoyed the tunes, during the rest of my drive to work. In that moment, I recognized my negativity and was able to overcome it. So no matter how much you work on being positive, there is always more to learn. I hope this book gives you the tools to venture off on your own journey of self-discovery for nipping your negative moments .

We wish you well on your quest to nip negativity in the butt and flip the tables of negative situations. Having a positive attitude about life will likely make you a happier person. Wouldn't this world be so much better with less negativity in it? While you might not be able to change the whole world, you can change your piece of the world.

We are confident you can make a difference and change your outlook, and maybe even a stranger's perception. Good luck and have fun! Life is too short not to be smiling as much as you possibly can!

Thank you, again.

Jeanie and Kris

Made in the USA
Columbia, SC
07 January 2020